business one : one

Rachel Appleby
John Bradley
Brian Brennan
Jane Hudson

student's book   pre-intermediate

OXFORD
UNIVERSITY PRESS

OXFORD
UNIVERSITY PRESS

Great Clarendon Street, Oxford OX2 6DP

Oxford University Press is a department of the University of Oxford.
It furthers the University's objective of excellence in research, scholarship,
and education by publishing worldwide in

Oxford New York

Auckland Cape Town Dar es Salaam Hong Kong Karachi
Kuala Lumpur Madrid Melbourne Mexico City Nairobi
New Delhi Shanghai Taipei Toronto

With offices in

Argentina Austria Brazil Chile Czech Republic France Greece
Guatemala Hungary Italy Japan Poland Portugal Singapore
South Korea Switzerland Thailand Turkey Ukraine Vietnam

OXFORD and OXFORD ENGLISH are registered trade marks of
Oxford University Press in the UK and in certain other countries

ISBN-13: 978 0 19 457640 6   Student's Book
ISBN-13: 978 0 19 457642 0   Student's Pack

Printed in China

ACKNOWLEDGEMENTS

The Business one:one pre-intermediate student's book was edited by Alastair
Lane.

The Business one:one MultiROM was written by Bill and Barbara Cheesman,
Gareth Davies, and Shaun Wilden.

Many thanks to Alastair Lane, families and friends, and all our colleagues in
Hungary and Spain who have contributed in one way or another to make this
book work.

The Business one:one glossary was produced by Rosalind Combley, with
definitions based on the Oxford Business English Dictionary for learners of
English, © Oxford University Press 2005 and the Oxford Advanced Learner's
Dictionary 7th edition, © Oxford University Pres 2005.

*The authors and publisher would like to thank the following people for giving permission
to reproduce interviews*: Annette Dalsgaard, Aysegul Kina, Ewa Krosnicka, Ingrid
Marcela Jara, Sue Gardiner, Mészáros Ágnes and Czigány Ildikó.

Art editing: Suzanne Williams / Pictureresearch.co.uk

Illustrations by: Ian Baker/CartoonStock pp 4, 10, 28, 53, 66; Annie Boberg/The
Organisation pp 16, 48; Mark Duffin p 40; Bill Ledger pp 8, 14, 30, 44, 47, 80,
82; Martin Sanders/Mapart p 79; Paul Oakley pp 12, 18, 22, 46, 54, 72, 76.

*We would also like to thank the following for permission to reproduce the following
photographs*: Alamy pp 18 (Robert Harding Picture Library Ltd), 20 (clocking
in/Stockbyte Platinum), (staff meeting/Lou Linwei), 36 (lavender/Edward
Parker), 38 (isifa Image Service s.r.o.), 42 (Tibor Bognar), 48 (Benno de Wilde/
Imageshop), 52 (RubberBall), 62 (Scott Hortop), 68 (zen garden/Tibor Bognar),
(riverbank and trees/Goncalo Diniz), 70 (arrivals/The Flight Collection), 78
(The Angel of the North/Roger Coulam), 82 (Molly Horn), 87 (kolvenbach),
93 (Bob Johns/expresspictures.co.uk), 101 (Eitan Simanor), 104 (PSL Images);
Axiom p 68 (women and Taj Mahal/Dinesh Khanna), (horses/Ian Cumming);
BAA Aviation Photolibrary p 70 (customs/In-Press: Steve Bates); Courtesy of
Karl Bushby/Goliath Expedition p 105a; Corbis pp 6 (Royalty-Free/Corbis),
26 (Royalty-Free/Corbis), 35 (Rahat Dar/epa), 74 (pastilla/Winkelmann/
photocuisine), 75 (Sergio Pitamitz), 78 (Sage/Richard Klune), 84 (Helen King),
90 (Jean-Philippe Arles), 98 (Rudolph Valentino/Bettmann); Courtesy of
Gergely Czigány p 107 (Ildiko Czigany); Empics pp 9 (Associated Press), 97
(Diane Bondareff/AP), 98 (Fabio Casatelli/Lionel Cirroneau/AP); Getty Images
pp 4 (Ryan McVay), 10 (DAJ), 12 (Stockbyte), 17 (Wide Group), 23 (Flying
Colours Ltd/Digital Vision), 24 (Hugh Sitton), 28 (Wide Group), 34 (Martin
Puddy), 36 (almonds/Mark McLane), (mint/Studio Paggy/IZA Stock), (aloe/
Wally Eberhart), (olives/Nicole Duplaix), 37 (Trinette Reed/Photographer's
Choice), 50 (Eric Audras/PhotoAlto), 54 (Patrick Ryan), 64 (Stockbyte), 66
(Jack Hollingsworth/Photodisc Green), 68 (Grand Canyon/Laura Ciapponi),
70 (Immigration officer/Digital Vision), (baggage reclaim/Jerry Driendl), 73
(Nicolas Russell), 74 (tajine/Jean Cazals), (chicken couscous/Louise Lister),
77 (Guy Vanderelst), 81 (Jerry Alexander), 88 (Eric Audras/PhotoAlto), 94
(Andreas Pollok), 98 (Eva Perón/Keystone/Stringer/Hulton Archive), (Charlie
Parker/Herman Leonard/Hulton Archive), 108 (Carl De Souza/AFP), 109 (Jan
Stromme); The National Trust Picture Library p 68 (flowers/Andrew Butler);
Courtesy of Nokia p 55; Rex Features p 32 (legs/Image Source), (Mexican resort/
Patrick Frilet); Still Pictures p 60 (ullstein/Unkel)

course syllabus

How to **say hello and goodbye**

01

In this lesson you will learn language for meeting people and introducing them to others.

Starter

1   Look at the questions below. Which ones can you ask when you meet someone for the first time in English-speaking countries?

   - Where are you from?
   - What is your first name?
   - How old are you?
   - Do you have any children?
   - What is the weather like in your country now?
   - How much do you earn?
   - Are you married?

2   Can you ask all these questions when you meet someone for the first time in your country? Which questions are not OK?

Expressions

1   Design4all is running a training course in Cairo. The participants meet on Sunday night to get to know each other. They meet again to say goodbye at the end of the week. Look at the two conversations. Find six mistakes in each conversation.

Hey, Jenny! Good to see you again.

Jordi, hi. I didn't expect to see you here. How are you?

Thanks, fine. And you?

Not bad. Is Tim coming too?

No. He can't come.

That's a shame. Ah look, here's Asim. Hi there. Do you know each other? Jordi – this is Asim Khan. He's from Karachi.

Hi. Nice to meet you.

Nice to meet you too. When did you get to here?

About an hour ago. And you?

I came early today morning … and this is Safina. She works here in Cairo. I'm sorry, what you did say your name was?

I'm Jordi. From Barcelona. Good to meet you. Jenny and I were on Gary's course in London last year. Have you met Gary?

No, not yet. But I've heard a lot about him.

Well, let me introduce you. He's just over there …

Er … Gary. Can I introduce you with Safina?

Hi, Safina. How are you? Ah yes – you did the online designs. It's nice to put a face to the name at last!

Pleased to meet you.

Do you like something to drink?

Thank you. Um, yes, an orange juice, please.

Speaking

1   You are at a conference. During the coffee break, you introduce a new contact (your teacher) to two colleagues. Later, you explain why you are leaving early. Role-play the conversations with your teacher.

IAN BAKER.

" HAVE YOU MET RUTH?.."

Writing

1   You receive an email from an international magazine, asking for information about what to do when you meet people in your country. Write an email in reply. Include:

   - how to greet people for the first time
   - how to greet members of the opposite sex
   - one or two greeting phrases from your language
   - what to do when saying goodbye
   - one or two phrases from your language to say goodbye
   - information on when people give gifts.

Hint

You can use **Good evening** when you want to say **Hello** at night.
You can use **Goodnight** when you want to say **Goodbye** at night.

"I'm afraid it gets late. I really must to go. The taxi's waiting outside.

OK. It was a great week, wasn't it?

Very good – especially the pyramids.

Yes. Don't forget to send me the photos.

No, I won't. Take care, Jenny. Bye.

Yes. Keep in touch and say hi to Tim from me.

Of course. See you, then, and goodbye, Safina.

Goodbye, Jordi. Have a good travel. It was great to meet you.

Bye, everyone!

So, Jenny, when you leave?

My flight is at six, so … not for a while.

Well, please to visit us here again one day. Gary!

Safina, hi.

I just wanted to say … Thanks everything. It was a great course.

Not at all. Thank you for telling us about the project. And are you in Dubai next month?

Yes, for the regional team meeting.

Well, I'll send you the schedule next week. See you then. All the best!

I'll look forward to seeing you again. Goodbye."

2 Listen to the conversations and check you found the six mistakes in each one.

3 Complete the sentences with the words used for meeting people.

1 Hi there! Do you know _____?

2 Jordi – _____ Asim Khan.

3 It's nice to be able to put a _____ the name at last!

4 I really _____ go. The taxi's waiting outside.

5 Take _____, Jenny. Bye!

6 Yes. Keep _____. Say hi to Tim from me!

7 Of course. _____ then and goodbye, Safina!

8 Well, I'll send you the schedule next week. See you then. _____!

Language box

Some phrases always use the same form of the verb. There are three groups.

The full infinitive:

I expect **to receive** the report tomorrow.

The *-ing* form (the gerund):

Thank you for **sending** the information.

The bare infinitive (without *to*)

I really must **go**.

Notice that the full infinitive often follows some adjectives – *pleased*, *nice*, *good*, etc.

Pleased **to meet** you.

Nice **to hear from** you.

Look

Look again at listening script 1.1 on page 113. Find more examples of the infinitive and *-ing*.

Lesson record

3 new words from this lesson

1 ....
2 ....
3 ....

3 useful phrases from this lesson

1 ....
2 ....
3 ....

Things to remember

....
....
....
....
....
....

How to **make offers**

02

In this lesson you will learn language for making, accepting, and refusing offers and suggestions.

Starter

1 Match the words (1–6) with the definitions (a–f).

1 a negotiation
2 management
3 inflation
4 a union
5 a rise
6 bonus

a an organization that represents employees
b a meeting to find an agreement
c the people who run a company
d when something goes up
e when the prices in a country go up
f extra money given occasionally to workers

2 Are you a member of a union? Why? Why not?

Expressions

2.1 o 1

Listen to a negotiation between a union and the management of a company in Ireland. Write down:

a the inflation rate _____
b what the union want _____
c what the management offers _____ .

Speaking

1 Make suggestions for the situations below to your teacher. Try to make more than one suggestion.

1 You and your colleagues cannot use the room that is reserved for a meeting. Your office is free.

2 You are in a meeting that has been going on for three hours. You can see that people need a break.

3 Your company needs an interpreter for a dinner with a VIP guest from your country.

4 A colleague has to get to the airport to fly home, but there are no taxis or public transport at the moment.

5 A meeting has come to the point where your knowledge is needed.

Language box

To make a suggestion or an offer, we can use:

Let's start now.
Shall I start?
Why don't you start?
How about starting now?
What about starting now?
I'll start, if you like.
Would you like me to start?

Hint

Be careful with **salary**, **wages**, and **pay**.
salary: the fixed amount of money you get every month
wages: usually not a fixed amount of money, paid by the hour
pay: a general word for the money you get for your work

2 Listen again. Complete the sentences with the words used for making offers and suggestions.

1 But anyway, _____ what the union has to say.

2 _____ start, Pat?

3 Yes, _____ ?

4 And _____ a bonus?

5 Pat, Maureen, _____ a pay rise the same as inflation.

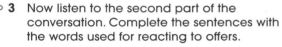

2.2 ○ 3 Now listen to the second part of the conversation. Complete the sentences with the words used for reacting to offers.

1 There's _____ we can pay 5.2%.

2 Sorry Josie, _____ just one payment here?

3 Hmm, _____ .

4 I think _____ .

5 We'll _____ your offer.

Writing

1 Write an answer to the email below. Try to use words and phrases from **Expressions** and the **Language box**.

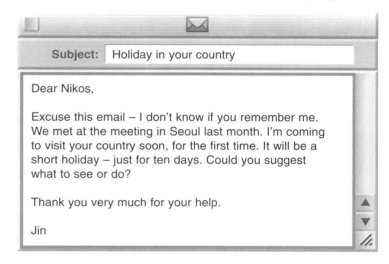

Subject: Holiday in your country

Dear Nikos,

Excuse this email – I don't know if you remember me. We met at the meeting in Seoul last month. I'm coming to visit your country soon, for the first time. It will be a short holiday – just for ten days. Could you suggest what to see or do?

Thank you very much for your help.

Jin

To react to an offer or a suggestion, some of the expressions we can use are:

There's no way we'd accept that.
(= this is a very direct *no*)

Do you mean Wednesday or Thursday?
(= asking for clarification)

That's not a bad idea.
(= positive, but careful, reaction)

I think it's a great idea.
(= enthusiastic reaction)

Look

Look again at listening script 2.1 on page 113. Find more examples of suggestions, offers, and reacting to suggestions and offers.

Lesson record

3 new words from this lesson	3 useful phrases from this lesson
1	**1** ....
2	**2** ....
3	**3** ....

Things to remember

....
....
....
....
....
....

How to **offer help**

03

In this lesson you will learn language for offering to help someone.

Starter

1 Have you ever been to a trade fair? Tell your teacher about it.

2 Find these words in the picture: *stand, poster, visitor, exhibitor, brochure, box*.

Expressions

3.1

1 Fran and John work for a travel guide publisher. They have a stand at a trade fair in London. Read the sentences below, and then listen to four short dialogues. Correct the information in the sentences. One of the sentences is already correct.

1 Fran cannot find the books on Australia.
2 Fran thinks there is space in the car for everything.
3 Fran has made a mistake with her T-shirt.
4 Fran does not want to go to the pub.

2 Now listen again. At each stage John is trying to help Fran. Does she accept his help?

Stage	Does Fran accept help?
1 In the office	
2 At the car	
3 Setting up the stand	
4 The end of the trade fair	

Speaking

1 A colleague from New York will be working in your department for three months. Your manager wants you to show them round this afternoon. Look at the list below. Is there anything else they need to see or know?

- members of staff
- departments / offices
- meeting rooms
- where to get help (IT, stationery, etc.)
- contact information for important clients
- kitchen (tea, coffee)
- lunch places

2 Decide on the order in which you want to do these things. Then tell your plans to your colleague (your teacher).

Language box

When offering help, there may be several things to do. To order activities, we can use the following phrases:

First / Firstly / First of all, …

Then / Next / Afterwards / After that, …

Finally / At the end, …

First of all, copy the file you want to the desktop. Then put the blank CD into the computer. After that, open the burner program. Then follow the instructions on the screen. Finally, check that the new CD works.

Hint

A **freebie** is something you get for nothing.
Freebies is a word which is often used to talk about promotional gifts which companies give away, e.g. pens, T-shirts.

3 Put the words from the dialogues in the correct order. Then listen again to check your answers.

1 want / help / you / do / some?

2 them / just / I'll / get.

3 help / me / let.

4 me / to / it / leave.

5 OK / doing / you / are?

6 want / hand / you / do / a?

7 can / how / help / I?

8 get / for / one / shall / you / I?

Writing

1 You have received the email below. Write a reply to say how you can help with:

- publicity (send out emails about the conference, put up posters)
- speakers (contact people, suggest topics for talks)
- brochures (help with contents)
- boxes
- the stand.

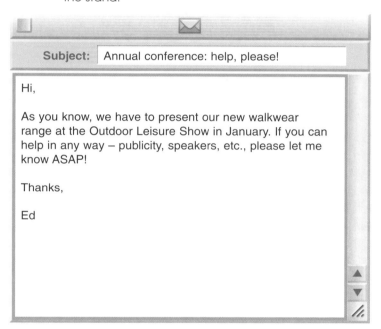

Subject: Annual conference: help, please!

Hi,

As you know, we have to present our new walkwear range at the Outdoor Leisure Show in January. If you can help in any way – publicity, speakers, etc., please let me know ASAP!

Thanks,

Ed

When talking about your own list of things to do, these phrases are usually followed by *I'll* ...:

First, I'll check my emails, and then I'll make some coffee. After that I'll write up the report, and finally, when it's finished, I'll send it to head office.

Look

Look again at listening script 3.1 on pages 113–114. Find more examples of offers and using *will* for a list of things to do.

Lesson record

3 new words from this lesson	3 useful phrases from this lesson
1	**1** ....
2	**2** ....
3	**3** ....

Things to remember

....

....

....

....

....

....

....

How to **check and clarify**

04

In this lesson you will learn language for checking and clarifying information.

Starter

1 Do you have a good memory or do you sometimes forget things? Do you use any of these things to help you remember?

- a diary
- a PDA (Personal Digital Assistant)
- Post-it notes
- a computer program
- a mobile phone

2 How do you organize a typical day at work?

Expressions

1 Read the email that Dave Jones received from his manager. What does Dave have to do? What does *clarify* mean?

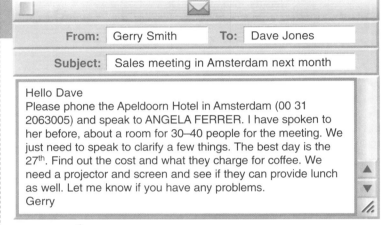

From:	Gerry Smith	To:	Dave Jones

Subject:	Sales meeting in Amsterdam next month

Hello Dave
Please phone the Apeldoorn Hotel in Amsterdam (00 31 2063005) and speak to ANGELA FERRER. I have spoken to her before, about a room for 30–40 people for the meeting. We just need to speak to clarify a few things. The best day is the 27th. Find out the cost and what they charge for coffee. We need a projector and screen and see if they can provide lunch as well. Let me know if you have any problems.
Gerry

4.1 ○ 2 Now listen to the phone conversation and complete Dave's notes.

> Apeldoorn Hotel – Angela Ferrer
> Room: _____ – can take _____ people   Cost _____
> Coffee break: _____ per person
> Lunch: _____ per person
> Projector / screen: yes / no
> Email for reservations: _____

" I'M SORRY BUT I THOUGHT IT WAS GOLF FIRST AND THEN THE MEETING. "

Speaking

1 Role-play the conversation between Dave Jones and Angela. Use the notes from **Expressions 1** and the information in the **Language box** to help you. Make sure that you check all your information.

2 Dave tells his boss about the details of the meeting in Amsterdam. Role-play the conversation. Your teacher will be Dave. You are the boss. You need to check:

- the room
- the dates
- the costs
- Angela's contact details.

Hint

Notice how these verbs are used:
Could you **repeat** ~~me~~ the question, please?
Could you **confirm** ~~me~~ the time of the meeting?
Can you **reserve** ~~me~~ a table for four people, please?

3 The following sentences are all used to check or clarify information. Complete sentences 1–8 with the words below.

do   please   other   whole
that   the   it   just

1   Could you _____ spell your company name for me, please?

2   Excuse me, was _____ thirteen or thirty?

3   Do you need the room for the _____ day?

4   Does that include tax, and all _____ costs?

5   _____ you mean a projector for transparencies or for a computer?

6   Sorry, could you repeat that, _____?

7   Yes. I'll spell _____ for you if you like.

8   When can you confirm _____ reservation, please?

4 Listen to 4.1 again to check your answers.

Writing

1 Write a question to check the information in sentences 1–9.

Example: The meeting starts at three o'clock.
          Sorry. What time did you say?
          Did you say two o'clock or three o'clock?

1   Can we meet next Wednesday instead?
2   I visit our clients in Manchester every four weeks.
3   It takes about five days to deliver to Holland.
4   Mr Petrovich is speaking at the conference.
5   Our new offices are about fifteen kilometres from the airport.
6   She decided to buy the biggest one.
7   The manager is going to Tokyo next week.
8   The new price is €125.
9   We didn't buy it because it was too expensive.

Look

Look again at listening script 4.1 on page 114. Find more examples of questions for checking information.

Language box

You can clarify things you do not hear or understand with a general question:

I'm sorry. What did you say?

If you want more specific clarification, use a different question word:

I'm sorry, what time did you say?
I'm sorry, how much did you say?
Excuse me, where did you say?

Another useful way to check information is simply to ask *Did you say?* and to repeat the information.

Did you say three o'clock?
Did you say twenty-five people?

Lesson record

3 new words from this lesson	3 useful phrases from this lesson
1	**1** ....
2	**2** ....
3	**3** ....

Things to remember

....
....
....
....
....
....

How to **start small talk**

05

In this lesson you will learn language for starting conversations with people you have not met before.

Starter

1 Look at the conversation topics. Do you talk about these topics in your country?
- the weather
- a typical day in my job
- the people I live with
- my journey to work

2 Choose a topic. Talk about it for a minute.

Expressions

1 Did you have a good flight?

2 Your flight was delayed, wasn't it?

3 You must be very tired. Shall we go straight to your hotel?

4 No, it's about twenty minutes, but it depends on the traffic?

5 What's the traffic like in Tokyo?

6 Yes, it's really warm. What's the weather like where you live?

Speaking

1 Role-play the following situations. Try to use language from **Expressions** and the **Language box**.

1 You arrive in Sydney, Australia for a meeting. Your colleague, Bruce Higgins, is picking you up from the airport. Your teacher, as Bruce Higgins, will start. See how long you can continue the conversation.

2 You are picking up a colleague, Yasmin Husseini, from her hotel. You want to make her feel comfortable, so start making small talk with her. Your teacher is Yasmin Husseini. See how long you can continue the conversation.

Writing

1 Read the email from a colleague who is going to visit your office. Write a suitable reply.

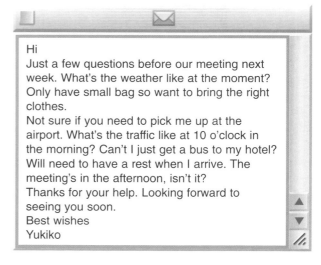

Hi
Just a few questions before our meeting next week. What's the weather like at the moment? Only have small bag so want to bring the right clothes.
Not sure if you need to pick me up at the airport. What's the traffic like at 10 o'clock in the morning? Can't I just get a bus to my hotel? Will need to have a rest when I arrive. The meeting's in the afternoon, isn't it?
Thanks for your help. Looking forward to seeing you soon.
Best wishes
Yukiko

dealing with people

Hint

Use the question **What is / are ... like?** in small talk.
What's the traffic like in Tokyo?
It's terrible, especially in the rush hour.
What are the houses like in Rio?
People live in flats, mostly.

1 The picture shows Danilo da Sousa meeting Yukiko Tomioka at Rio de Janeiro international airport. Match Yukiko's comments (a–f) with Danilo's comments in the picture (1–6).

a Yes, please. I'd like to have a rest.

b It's a lovely day, isn't it?

c Yes. We were delayed for an hour in Tokyo.

d Well, it wasn't too bad.

e It's terrible, especially in the rush hour.

f The hotel isn't far, is it?

2 Write the expressions in the correct place under the three headings on the right.

• People work very long hours here, don't they?

• It was raining hard.

• What do people wear to work?

• It's very windy, isn't it?

• It took us two hours to get here.

• It snows a lot here, doesn't it?

• The plane was delayed for an hour.

• Nobody studies languages where I come from.

• How was your flight?

• Most people live in flats in the centre.

• Was someone waiting for you when you arrived?

• Is it always so hot here?

Talking about your journey

1 _____

2 _____

3 _____

4 _____

Talking about the weather

1 _____

2 _____

3 _____

4 _____

Talking about your country

1 _____

2 _____

3 _____

4 _____

Language box

We use question tags at the end of a sentence to check information or make small talk. If the sentence is positive, the tag is negative:

It**'s** a long flight, **isn't it**?
You **were** late, **weren't you**?

If the sentence is negative, the tag is positive:

Your bags **aren't** heavy, **are they**?
The plane **wasn't** full, **was it**?

We can also form question tags with *can*, *have*, and *will*:

He **can't drive, can he**?
She**'s got** a dog, **hasn't she**?
They**'ll give** us lunch, **won't they**?

Look

Look again at **Expressions**. Find more examples of question tags.

Lesson record

3 new words from this lesson	3 useful phrases from this lesson
1	**1** ....
2	**2** ....
3	**3** ....

Things to remember

....

....

....

....

....

....

How to **describe an event**

06

In this lesson you will learn language for explaining something that happened to you.

Starter

1 What is happening in the picture?

6.1 ○ **2** Listen to this conversation in an office. What are they talking about?

Expressions

6.2 ○ **1** Mark, Gina, and Simon are talking during a coffee break at their office in New York. Listen and answer the questions.

1. Why was Simon in London?
2. What was the problem at Heathrow Airport?
3. What did the airline staff ask the passengers?
4. What did Simon say?

6.3 ○ **2** Listen to the final part of the conversation. Put the questions in the correct order and answer them.

1. second / he / did / what / say / time / the?
2. the / staff / to / proposal / did / his / airline / agree?
3. things / three / Simon / get / did / what?

6.2 ○ **3** Listen again to the earlier part of the conversation. Correct the sentences with the verb forms used for telling a story.

1. I was in London a few years ago on a business trip, and flew back home.
2. I could see these two ground staff – they came down the line.
3. Well, I can see that there were families on vacation ...

Speaking

1 Tell your teacher about a problem that you had while travelling.

- Where were you travelling to / from?
- Why were you travelling?
- What was the problem?
- How did you feel?
- Who did you talk to?
- How was it resolved?
- How did you feel afterwards?

2 Role-play a situation at the airport, like Simon's. Ask for compensation. Try to use language from **Expressions** and the **Language box** for how to describe an event.

Language box

If an adjective has one syllable, add *-er than* to make the comparative:

This model is **newer than** the one you're using.

Your presentation should be **shorter than** ten minutes.

The flight will be **longer than** three hours.

Two important exceptions are *good* and *bad*:

I think your new office is much **better than** the old one.

The heating system is **worse than** it was before, I'm afraid.

If an adjective ends in *-y* and has two syllables, replace the *-y* with *-ier*:

Careful! This is **heavier than** you think.

You seem **happier than** you did last week.

Hint

Would you mind is common for polite requests. The verb for the request takes the gerund form.
Would you mind flying tomorrow instead of today?

Hint

Notice the answer to **would you mind**.
Would you mind waiting here, madam?
No, I wouldn't (mind). (= that is not a problem)
Actually, I would (mind). (= that is a problem, I do not agree)

4   … and they probably have had a tighter schedule than me.

5   And I went home, so a day earlier, a day later, what the heck.

6   No, I was saying: 'It would be very inconvenient for me …'

6.3 **4   Put the words from the dialogue in the correct order. Then listen again to the final part of the conversation to check your answers.**

1   guess / and / what? They couldn't find anyone else …

2   knew / I / if / back / came / they, the situation would be worse.

3   so / told / them / I: 'As I said before, it's not convenient for me to miss this flight, but …'

4   finished / not / on / I'm / yet / hang.

5   do / think / what / you? They agreed immediately.

6   Well / phoned / told / home / I / and / wife / my …

Writing

1   You work for an airline that uses local hotels when it has overbooked flights. Write a report for your boss comparing the two hotels below. Recommend one of the hotels to use when flights are overbooked.

> The Emperor, usually very quiet, beautiful hotel, good restaurant and business facilities, small gym, staff very helpful when there's a problem.

> The Royal, some street noise, excellent restaurant, poor business facilities, no gym, staff not very helpful when there's a problem.

For most adjectives with two or more syllables, add *more … than*:

> Their idea is **more expensive** and **more complicated than** ours.

Or *less … than* to make the negative:

> This kind of problem is **less frequent than** before.

Look

Look again at listening scripts 6.1–6.3 on page 114. Find more examples of comparatives.

Lesson record

3 new words from this lesson	3 useful phrases from this lesson
1	**1** ....
2	**2** ....
3	**3** ....

Things to remember

....
....
....
....
....
....

How to **talk about yourself**

In this lesson you will learn language for giving information about yourself and your work.

Starter

1 Look at the picture. Is your office like this?

2 What is the biggest time problem you have?

3 What's your busiest time of the week? And of the year?

Expressions

7.1 ○ 1 Susan is starting a new job and she meets her new manager, Melissa. Listen and complete the notes that Susan takes at the meeting.

> Start work at _____
> First thing _____
> Melissa in office on _____
> Usually visits clients on _____
> Prefers to visit clients _____
> Planning meeting every _____
> Sales meeting on _____
> Presentations _____
> Trips abroad in total _____
> Finish work at _____

7.2 ○ 2 Later Susan has lunch with one of her new colleagues, Cathy. Listen for the answers to the following questions.

1 What is Melissa's job?

2 Where is Susan from?

3 Why does Cathy go to Tenerife twice a year?

Speaking

1 Imagine that your teacher is your new assistant. Role-play a similar conversation to **Expressions 1** and tell your teacher about your work. Include information about the following:

- timetable
- routine jobs
- meetings
- travelling
- clients.

Language box

To talk about frequency, use the following adverbs. Notice their position in the sentences.

I **always** work in the garden at the weekend. (= every Saturday and Sunday)

We **never** close. We are **always** open. (= twenty-four hours a day, seven days a week)

It **often** rains here. (= this happens a lot)

She's **frequently** late for work. (= this happens a lot)

I **usually** have lunch at work. (= three or four times a week)

We **sometimes** work late. (= once or twice a week)

I **rarely** use my car in town (= not often)

Hint

Be careful with the pronunciation of the **s** /ɪz/ in the following verbs.
organize: **Cathy organizes her visits.**
arrange: **She arranges her appointments.**
supervise: **She supervises the office when her boss is away.**
manage: **Her boss manages the sales department.**

3 Match the questions (1–10) with the answers (a–j). Then listen again to check your answers.

1   Where shall we sit?
2   Where are you from, Susan?
3   Did you move here for the job?
4   Do you like living here?
5   What do you do in your spare time?
6   How often do you do that?
7   Do you visit your family often?   *c*
8   Does your family live in London?
9   Do you ever go and visit them?
10 Do you want some coffee?

a   I was born in Birmingham.
b   I like to do some sport. I run a little.
c   Yes, I go back home about once a month.
d   No, my mother and sister live in Tenerife.
e   Yes, please, but let me.
f   Two or three times a week.
g   Over there, near the window.
h   Yes, there are a lot of things to do.
i   Yes, but not for this one.
j   Yes, twice a year.

Writing

1 You are Susan. Write a short email to a friend describing your new manager and the new job. Begin your email like this.

Subject: New job!

I started my new job today. I work for the manager of the sales department. I start work at eight o'clock

To give more specific information about frequency, use these expressions:

He visits the office ... once a week.
once or twice a month.
two or three times a year.
every Monday.
every three months.

To ask about the frequency of an action, use the questions *How often* or *Do you often*:

How often do you travel for work?

Do you often travel for work?

Look

Look again at listening scripts 7.1 and 7.2 on pages 114–115. Find more examples of adverbs and expressions of frequency.

Lesson record

3 new words from this lesson	3 useful phrases from this lesson
1	1 ....
2	2 ....
3	3 ....

Things to remember

....
....
....
....
....
....

How to **talk about other people**

08

In this lesson you will learn language for describing people's appearance and personality.

Starter

1 Look at the picture. How would you feel in this situation?

2 What sort of social events do you go to for work?

Expressions

○ 1 SIB bank is having its annual international meeting in Funchal, Madeira. Suzanne and José are at the opening reception. Listen and (circle) the people in the picture they talk about.

2 Find these words in the picture: *high-heels, trainers, pullover, jeans, tie, trousers, waistcoat, glasses.*

Speaking

1 Look again at the picture of the reception in Funchal. Choose two or three people to describe, but do not tell your teacher which ones. Talk about what they are wearing, and see if your teacher can guess who you are talking about. Use some of the words below.

hair: long / medium-length / short / dark / black / dark brown / red / fair / straight / curly / wavy

build: tall / medium height / short / well-built (large) / medium build / slim / thin

extras: with a beard / bald

2 Think of three people you work with regularly, perhaps colleagues or clients. How would you describe their personality?

dealing with people

Hint

In this unit you hear a lot of British words for clothing.
American English uses some different words.

GB	US
trousers	pants
waistcoat	vest
trainers	sneakers
pullover	sweater

3 José and Suzanne talk about the following people. Match the people (1–5) with the descriptions (a–e). Then listen again to check your answers.

1 Antonio

2 Henri Joli

3 Paolo Rodrigues

4 Business development manager

5 Director for Austria

a a bit serious and distant

b quiet and rather shy

c rather smart / looks quite nice

d very open and friendly

e he's got a great sense of humour

4 Listen again and complete the sentences below with words used for descriptions.

1 He's the one over there talking to the woman _____.

2 And next to him there's a man

_____.

3 He's quite well-_____.

4 He seems much _____ I thought!

5 He's tall and thin, and _____.

Writing

1 A colleague from abroad will be arriving next week to visit you. You plan to meet them at the airport. You will be going straight from work. Write an email to them to describe what you look like, and what you will be wearing. Use the example below to help you.

Subject:	Meeting at the airport

Dear Miro,

I'm looking forward to seeing you next week.
I'll come to the airport to meet you.
I'm quite tall with dark hair and a moustache. I'll be wearing a black suit and I'll be carrying a blue bag.
I'm sure you'll find me!
Have a good journey!

Rudi Alvarez

Look

Look again at listening script 8.1 on page 115. Find more examples of *one, ones, this, that, these,* and *those.*

Language box

We can use *the one,* or *the ones* when we know what we are talking about.

He's **the one** talking to Maria. (i.e. the man)

They're **the ones** who went to Germany. (i.e. the people)

You can use *this, that, these,* and *those* to indicate if things are placed near to you, or far away from you.

This letter came for you yesterday. (= it is near)

That man over there works in Sales.
(= he is not near you)

These books are for you. (= they are near)

Those people are staying at the same hotel.
(= they are not near)

Lesson record

3 new words from this lesson	3 useful phrases from this lesson
1	**1** ....
2	**2** ....
3	**3** ....

Things to remember

....
....
....
....
....
....

How to talk about time

In this lesson you will learn language for giving information about time.

Starter

1   Do you do any of these things? How often?
  • take work home
  • work more than fifty hours a week
  • go into the office on Saturday
  • forget to take holidays
  • go to the office early
  • go without lunch
  • work late

Expressions

1   Tom is the manager of a small team at BAB Ltd, a medium-sized manufacturing company. The company has just announced new working conditions. Tom is reporting the news to his staff. Listen and mark the changes to the present timetable below.

bab ltd

Working conditions – Office staff

Timetable –

Working week	39 hours	
Working day	start 09.00	finish 18.00
Fridays	start 09.00	finish 17.00
Lunch break	Monday to Friday	
	Minutes 60	13.00 to 14.00

Holidays –

Christmas	National holidays + 3 days
Easter	National holidays + 2 days
Summer	20 holiday days
	July – September

Speaking

1   Complete these notes about the working conditions in your company or country and then explain them to your teacher. Ask your teacher questions about their working conditions. Are they the same?

Working week		hours	
Working day(s)	start	finish	
Lunch break		minutes	to
Coffee break	morning		afternoon
Holidays			
Annual number		working days	
Usual month(s)			
National holidays			

Hint

Be careful when saying and writing dates.
We say **the fifteenth of March** but we write 15th March.
We can also say **March the twenty-third** but we write March 23rd.

9.2

2 Listen to the next part of the meeting. What does Tom say about holidays? There is one question at the end of the meeting. What is the question and what is Tom's answer?

3 Put the words from the dialogues in the correct order. Then listen again to check your answers.

1 have / the / number / we / same / of / days.

2 July or August / twenty / days / we / have / to take / now / the complete / in.

3 holidays / some / year / of / took / us / in / September / last / our.

4 1st / these / on / start / conditions / next / new / January / year.

5 between / you / twenty / take / can / for coffee / minutes / 10.00 and 12.00.

Writing

1 A friend is thinking about working in your company. Write an email explaining the working conditions. Give information about these points in your email:

• working week
• working day
• coffee and lunch breaks
• meetings
• company and national holidays.

Look

Look again at listening scripts 9.1 and 9.2 on pages 115–116. Find more examples of time prepositions.

Language box

We use different prepositions when speaking about time.

Parts of the day:	in the morning, afternoon, evening at night
Months:	in January, February
Seasons:	in spring, summer, autumn, winter
Years:	in 1996
Days and dates:	on Monday, on June 22nd
Public holiday periods:	at Christmas
Specific times:	at half past seven at 12.00, at midday at midnight

Length of times:

The meeting is **from** 10.00 **to** 12.00.
There is a break **between** 10.00 **and** 14.00.

Lesson record

3 new words from this lesson	3 useful phrases from this lesson
1	1 ....
2	2 ....
3	3 ....

Things to remember

....
....
....
....
....

How to talk about a past project

In this lesson you will learn language for talking about a past project.

Starter

1 When do you buy things?

a   When you get a 'cold call' at home?

b   When a salesman visits your house?

c   When you receive publicity at home?

d   On the Internet?

e   When you see something very cheap?

f   When watching TV shopping channels?

Expressions

10.1

1 It is seven in the evening when Leonard Wareham receives a phone call. Listen and answer the questions.

1   Who is calling? Why?

2   What is Leonard's reaction?

2 Isabel works for Spotlight, an advertising agency. One of her clients is Portugal Homes, a property development company, selling holiday homes in the Algarve. She gives a report of the recent campaign to her colleagues. Look at her presentation notes and put them in the correct order.

Action	When
1 Portugal Homes contacted Spotlight	May
Cold calling	
The first Sales Evening	
Prepared the advertising	
Presented the proposal	
2 Visited the client and had meetings	

10.2

2 Listen and check your answers and complete the *When* section.

Speaking

1 Tell your teacher about projects that you have finished at work (or at home) recently. Use questions 1–8 to help you.

1   What exactly was the project? What did you want to do?

2   Did you need any help from anyone else?

3   What did you do first?

4   What were two or three important moments in the project?

5   How long was the project and when did you finish?

6   How many people worked on the project?

7   What kind of budget did you have?

8   Are you happy with the results?

Language box

Use the past simple to speak about finished or completed actions in the past. We often say when the action happened.

I **went** to the conference in May.

They **phoned** my office yesterday.

Use the present perfect to speak about actions that started in the past and continue in the present.

I **have been** to three conferences this year.

They **have phoned** a lot of people this month.

projects

Hint

Use the past form of **have to** for a past obligation.
Did you **have to** change the budget?
We **had to** finish the project in December.

10.3 **4** Isabel now answers questions from her colleagues. Listen and complete the sentences.

1 Did you have to change the _____ ?

2 Did you finish the project _____ ?

3 Just! We had to finish the campaign for the _____ in December.

4 Is the client _____ with the _____ ?

5 Yes, they are. Sales have increased _____ %. They have sold _____ than 350 holiday homes since January this year.

6 **Voice 3** Have you finished your work with the client?

   Isabel Not _____ .

Writing

1 You work for Spotlight. Isabel asks you to write a summary of the Portugal Homes campaign with information about the results. Take the information you need from **Expressions**. Write about 100 words.

Compare the following sentences.

Did you meet the client last week? (= There was a meeting. This meeting is finished.)

Have you met the client before? (= Is this, or will this be, your first meeting with the client?)

They visited six countries last year. (= Last year is finished. The number of countries is final and cannot change.)

They have visited more than eight countries since January this year. (= They can visit more countries – the number might increase.)

Look

Look again at listening scripts 10.2 and 10.3 on page 116. Find more examples of the past simple and the present perfect tenses.

Lesson record

3 new words from this lesson

1 ....

2 ....

3 ....

3 useful phrases from this lesson

1 ....

2 ....

3 ....

Things to remember

....
....
....
....
....
....
....

How to **talk about money**

In this lesson you will learn language for talking about money.

Starter

1 What would you do with:

€10,000?	€75,000?	€500,000?
retire?	invest it?	move house?
spend it?	buy a new car?	give it away?

2 Are you good with money? Do you:
- have a credit card?
- check your bank statements?
- pay bills on time?
- have a weekly or monthly budget?

Expressions

Think business, Think Malta.

An exclusive development of office property situated next to the new Malta Yacht Marina.

For more information contact:
Tel: +356 2292 4570
Mail: Malta Yacht Marina Development,
137 Independence Square, Valletta, Malta

11.1 ○ 1 John and David started their own company, AH Marine Services Ltd, in 1990. They specialize in insuring and chartering boats. John is looking for new offices in Malta. Listen and answer the questions.

1 Where are the new offices?
2 What's the problem with the new offices?
3 How much do they cost?
4 What's David's reaction?
5 How does John feel?

Writing

1 You are David. You telephoned the bank and made an appointment for Wednesday, 11.00 a.m. Write an email to confirm it and explain why you want to speak to them.

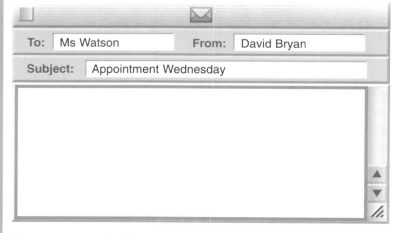

To:	Ms Watson	From:	David Bryan
Subject:	Appointment Wednesday		

Speaking

1 Role-play the conversation between David and the bank manager. AH Marine Services Ltd has been a good client of the bank for five years. You want information about the cost of a loan for €150,000 over seven years. The bank manager (your teacher) is going to ask you:
- why you need new offices
- some information about the new offices you have seen
- how much capital you have
- how much money you will need
- why you are going to buy and not rent the new offices.

2 Now listen to the next part of the conversation. Mark the sentences true (T) or false (F).

1 David wants to buy the new offices. _____

2 They will need less than a quarter of a million euros from the bank. _____

3 John will speak to the bank manager. _____

3 Match 1–6 with a–f to make complete sentences. Then listen to the second part of the conversation again to check your answers.

1 We were thinking of a monthly rent
2 We agreed on a budget of €100,000
3 We don't need to spend our money
4 I'm sure the bank will give us a loan
5 Buying our own offices would be
6 Property is increasing in price

a on building work or decoration.
b by over fifteen per cent a year at the moment.
c a good investment for the future.
d in the region of six to seven thousand euros.
e for the rest of the capital.
f for possible building and decoration costs.

4 Complete this summary of the situation with the words below.

rent   budget   investment
loan   capital

The new offices will be a big
¹ _____ for the company.
They will need a ² _____
from the bank, because they don't
have the necessary ³ _____
themselves. Their original idea was
to pay a monthly ⁴ _____
and they had a ⁵ _____
of €100,000 for building and
decorating costs.

Language box

Look at how you say large numbers in English.

370,000 three hundred **and** seventy thousand
1,250 one thousand two hundred **and** fifty

How to speak generally, and to speak about fractions:

It costs just over / just under / around a million.
three quarters of a million

To express decimal numbers, use the word *point* **and say the numbers individually.**

8.95 eight point nine five
0.56 oh point five six

Look

Look again at listening scripts 11.1 and 11.2 on pages 116–117. Find more examples of numbers and percentages.

Lesson record

3 new words from this lesson	3 useful phrases from this lesson
1	1 ....
2	2 ....
3	3 ....

Things to remember

....
....
....
....
....
....

12

In this lesson you will learn language for describing a project.

Starter

1 What different stages do you follow when you get a new passport?

- have your photo / fingerprints taken?
- fill in a form?
- go to a government office?
- pay money?
- get a reference?

2 Is there anything else you need to do?

Expressions

1 Read the magazine article about MTC and answer the questions.

1 What do MTC and BBA stand for?
2 Where is the new centre?
3 Who are the partners?
4 What will the new centre do?

New company on the park

The new Materials Test Centre, MTC, was officially opened last Friday in the Tyne Technology Park, Newcastle. The new centre is the result of a joint venture between local companies, the Industrial Development Board and the British Builders Association. The main aim of the centre is to test new building materials. Set up two years ago following an initiative by

2 Read the rest of the article. Mark the sentences true (T) or false (F).

1 The new test lines are twice as fast as the older methods. _____
2 The new cost of testing will be less than half what it is now. _____
3 The company will be making a profit in about a year. _____

Speaking

1 Use the information from **Expressions** and the following slide to present the MTC project to your teacher. You may like to look again at listening script 12.1 on page 117 before you do this activity. A tick (✓) indicates the stage is complete.

MTC PROJECT

Stages

1 Business plan, funding, construction work ✓

2 Production lines + offices + laboratories ✓

3 Testing machinery, training staff   Delayed (three weeks)

4 Full capacity   On schedule

Language box

Use the verb *to be able to* instead of *can* when you want to talk about the ability to do something in the past:

I missed the first flight but I **was able to** catch a later one.

They **weren't able to** deliver yesterday because of the strike.

Or in the future:

The doctor says I'**ll be able to** come back to work at the end of the month.

Don't worry. We'**re going to be able to** fix the problem.

projects

Hint

When talking about financial plans, use the following expressions:

to make a profit (positive)
to make a loss (negative)
to cover costs (no losses but no profits)
to break even (to reach a point where you are covering costs).

MTC, the Materials Testing Centre, will be fully operational in twelve months' time. The centre will be able to test a wide range of new materials that are used in the construction industry.

The new automated test lines will be able to test new materials in a quarter of the time used by more traditional methods. This means the BBA will be able to reduce the costs of these tests by as much as 70%. As a result, MTC expect to be able to cover operating costs in twelve months and to break even in less than two years from now

12.1 **3** Now listen to two conversations between Diana Walker, technical manager of MTC, and her manager, Mark Darling. The first conversation is in May and the second one in June. Listen and answer the questions.

1 How many different project stages does Diana mention in total?

2 What was the problem with a delay?

3 In the second conversation, is the project better or worse?

4 When does the production phase begin?

Writing

12.1 **1** Correct the sentences below. Then listen again to check your answers.

1 The automated test lines: can you bring me on to date on them?

2 Are they going to be finished as plan?

3 Yes. We're behind of schedule by about three weeks.

4 It was only a two-weeks delay in the end.

5 We expect to be back to schedule very soon.

6 When will the centre be all operational?

2 Think of a project at work. Write a short report describing this project. Include the following information:

• when and why you started the project

• what you wanted to do and what you were able to do

• what you are doing now

• what you will be able to do in the future.

And with an infinitive or a modal verb:

They **expect to be able to** arrive before twelve o'clock.

He **should be able to** solve the problem for you.

Look

Look again at listening script 12.1 on page 117 and the article about MTC in **Expressions**. Find more examples of *be able to*.

Lesson record

3 new words from this lesson	3 useful phrases from this lesson
1	1 ....
2	2 ....
3	3 ....

Things to remember

....
....
....
....
....
....

How to talk about personnel

13

In this lesson you will learn language for talking about personnel.

Starter

1 Number the steps for employing a new person in your company.

    _____ contact recruitment agency
    _____ interview candidates
    _____ select candidates
       1   write job description
    _____ make final decision
       2   advertise new post
    _____ decide conditions
    _____ sign a contract

Expressions

13.1

1 Isabel works for an advertising agency, Spotlight. She is preparing an offer for Italia Tours. They organize holidays in Italy and want to do some promotion in the UK. Isabel is speaking to her manager, Tony. Listen to their conversation and answer the questions.

1 Did Isabel have a good weekend?
2 Is the Italia Tours contract important?
3 Why is Isabel worried?
4 When will she see her boss?

13.2

2 It is now Friday. Tony and Isabel have their meeting. Complete the sentences with the words below. Then listen and check your answers.

staff	work on	contract	experience
recruit	full-time	team	agency
take on	temporary		

Tony Congratulations about the Italia Tours contract! That's great news!

Isabel Thank you, but we need to
¹ _____ some more people –
and quickly.

Tony What ² _____ do you think
you need?

Speaking

1 Isabel wrote the graphic designer's job description. Prepare Tony's questions for Nicole, the designer. Then role-play the conversation with your teacher.

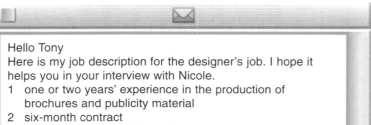

Hello Tony
Here is my job description for the designer's job. I hope it helps you in your interview with Nicole.
1 one or two years' experience in the production of brochures and publicity material
2 six-month contract
3 good spoken Italian if possible
4 willing to travel
5 familiar with design programs: Adobe InDesign and Quark XPress
6 likes working in a small team
Isabel

projects

Hint

There are many different types of working contracts.
full-time (all day or all year)
part-time (part of the day)
fixed term (for a specific period, e.g. nine months)
~~temporary~~ (for a limited period)

Isabel	Well, I think I need a ³ _____ of three people who can ⁴ work on this contract. We should ⁵ _____ one admin person who can help in the office. We can get someone from an ⁶ _____. A ⁷ _____ secretary with a six-month ⁸ _____.
Tony	What do you think? Should we look for someone ⁹ _____ or not?
Isabel	Yes, I think so. Someone who has three or four years' ¹⁰ _____.

13.3 **3** Now listen as Tony and Isabel continue their conversation. They're talking about one of their employees, Nicole. Why does Isabel recommend Nicole?

4 Correct the mistakes in the sentences. Then listen again to check your answers.

1 She's not very experience!

2 She's hard-work.

3 She's very create and imagination and she learns quickly.

4 And she's completely depend.

Writing

1 You have a lot of work at the moment and you need to employ a new person to work with you. Complete the following notes and then write a short email to your manager describing the person you need and why you need them.

Position: _____

Age: _____

Experience: _____

Languages: _____

Type of contract: _____

Look

Look again at listening script 13.2 on page 117. Find more examples of relative clauses with *who* and *that*.

Language box

When talking about people, we can combine two sentences using a relative clause with *who* or *that*.

We are looking for a new secretary. The person should have three years' experience.

We are looking for **a new secretary who (that) should have** three years' experience.

We want to employ a salesperson. This salesperson must speak Italian.

We want to employ **a salesperson who (that) must speak** Italian.

Jane is the accounts manager. She looks after three big contracts.

Jane is **the accounts manager who (that) looks after** three big contracts.

Lesson record

3 new words from this lesson	3 useful phrases from this lesson
1	1 ....
2	2 ....
3	3 ....

Things to remember

....
....
....
....
....
....

How to **talk about project stages**

In this lesson you will learn language for talking about project stages.

Starter

1 Think of a popular product for each item in the list. Then discuss the questions with your teacher.

- a magazine
- a chocolate bar
- a breakfast food
- a soft drink

1 What is the brand name of the product?

2 Is it expensive?

3 How is it advertised? (on TV? the radio? in newspapers and magazines?)

4 Do you use it yourself?

Expressions

14.1 ○ 1 Jane and Mike work in advertising, organizing publicity campaigns. Jane was working with a client called McKinley, a manufacturer of a new juice drink called *Kiwi Kool*. Listen to their conversation and answer the questions.

1 Is the McKinley campaign finished?

2 Did Jane like working with the client? Why / Why not?

Writing

1 You are Jane's colleague, Mike. Look at the email your boss sent you. Write a reply.

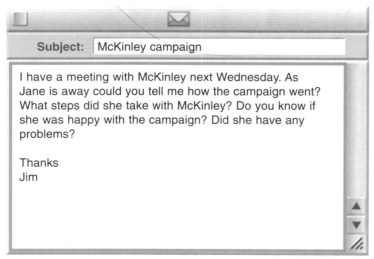

Subject: McKinley campaign

I have a meeting with McKinley next Wednesday. As Jane is away could you tell me how the campaign went? What steps did she take with McKinley? Do you know if she was happy with the campaign? Did she have any problems?

Thanks
Jim

Language box

We use the past simple to talk about finished actions. We usually give a time reference.

They **started** the company in **1989**.

Did the documents **arrive this morning**?

We use the past continuous to talk about longer actions in the past. Perhaps these actions are unfinished or interrupted. It is often used with another past simple verb.

We waited in the hotel reception because they **were cleaning** our room.

What **were you doing** yesterday morning?

Other is used with plural nouns.
**That hotel is quite reasonable. The other hotels
are quite expensive.**
Another is used with singular nouns.
I think we have another problem.

14.2

2 Now listen to the rest of their conversation. Match the stages of the project (1–6) with the corresponding month (a–f).

1 present proposal   a January
2 launch product   b February
3 agree final plan   c March
4 meet client   d April
5 cut TV campaign   e May
6 sign contract   f June

3 Put the words from the dialogue in the correct order. Then listen again to check your answers.

1 step / was / to / the / meet / first / client / in / January / the.
2 next / prepare / the / was / step / to / publicity / the.
3 25% / budget / by / they / the / cut.
4 worried / our / I / deadline / was / because / the / was / end / May / of.
5 we / going / to / the / supermarkets / were / launch / product / shops / and / at.
6 only / final / May / agreed / in / we / the / plan / on.

Speaking

1 Make four sentences from the table.

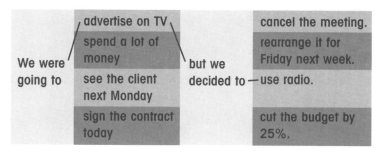

2 Make four sentences from the table. This time add some extra information.

Example: I was going to look for a new job but I decided to speak to the manager instead. He offered me a different job with better conditions.

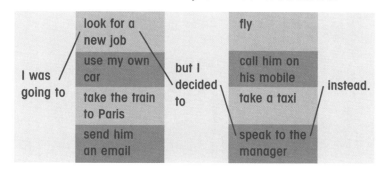

We use *was / were going to* to speak about a change of plan in the past.

I **was going** to leave the office early today but just look at the time!
(= I did not leave early)

I thought **you were going to** phone me!
(= Why didn't you phone?)

I knew **he was going to say** that!
(= I expected him to say that)

Look

Look again at listening scripts 14.1 and 14.2 on pages 117–118. Find more examples of the different past tenses.

Lesson record

3 new words from this lesson   3 useful phrases from this lesson

1 ....   1 ....
2 ....   2 ....
3 ....   3 ....

Things to remember

....
....
....
....
....
....

How to talk about future projects

15

In this lesson you will learn language for talking about future projects.

Starter

1 **What is your idea of a perfect holiday?**

on the beach
doing some sport
relaxing in a nice place

sightseeing
in the countryside
staying at home

Expressions

15.1

1 The Royal Hotel Group is building a new hotel complex on the Riviera Maya in Mexico. William is the manager of the project and Tony is the managing director of the company. Listen to their conversation and complete the notes that Tony takes during the call.

RIVIERA MAYA ROYAL HOTEL – schedule?

1 Important building work? – December this year

2 Decoration / gardens / swimming pool? – _____

3 Recruiting / training new staff? – _____

4 First reservations? – _____

5 Full capacity? – _____

Tony – retiring _____

Employ new assistant manager as of _____

Speaking

1 **What will you be doing, and what do you think will be happening in five, ten, or fifteen years' time? Discuss the following personal and general points with your teacher.**

the same company?

retiring at fifty-five?

the same hobbies?

working from home with a computer?

working thirty hours a week?

the same job?

projects

Hint

to be on time – to arrive or to happen punctually
The meeting started on time. (The agreed time was 16.00 and it started at 16.00.)

Hint

to be (just) in time – to arrive or happen before the deadline for something
We got to the airport just in time to catch the plane. (We were almost too late.)

15.2

2 Now listen to the second conversation between Tony and William.

1 Why does Tony phone William?

2 What is the problem?

3 How does this affect the schedule?

3 Now listen to the second conversation again and match the beginning of each sentence (1–5) with the end (a–e).

1 I'm afraid _____

2 There's a group of local people _____

3 I'll be speaking to them _____

4 We won't be working on the gardens and _____

5 Everything else is fine _____

a next week about it.

b I've got some bad news.

c who are protesting about the plans.

d swimming pools until the end of January.

e and on schedule.

Writing

1 You are Tony. Your meeting with the local authorities went well. You have permission to start the work in the third week of January but you have to reduce the size of the swimming pool. This means a three-week delay. Write an email to William to tell him the news in the space below.

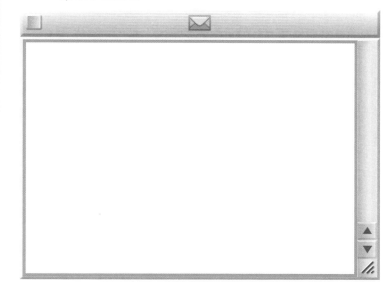

Look

Look again at listening scripts 15.1 and 15.2 on page 118. Find more examples of the future continuous.

Language box

Use the future continuous, *will be doing*, to express an action in progress at a specific time in the future.

Next year **we will be celebrating** our fiftieth anniversary.

They **will be working** in their new offices this time next year.

Phone me when you want. **I'll be working** in the office all morning.

You can also use the future continuous to make predictions:

All cars **will be using** hybrid motors twenty years from now.

I think we **will all be living** in enormous tower blocks in the future.

They'll be implanting mobile phones in our ears soon.

Lesson record

3 new words from this lesson

1 ....

2 ....

3 ....

3 useful phrases from this lesson

1 ....

2 ....

3 ....

Things to remember

....

....

....

....

....

How to **update**

16

In this lesson you will learn language for talking about tasks which are done, or not yet complete.

Starter

1   When you go to a new city, what do you like to see?

Expressions

16.1

1   Two-step Guides are bringing out a new edition of their guide to Pakistan. Charles has just come back from Lahore, and is talking to Gavin, the editor, about how to update each section. Listen to their conversation, and mark which sections are already complete (✓) and which are incomplete (✗).

Background	Sightseeing
Shopping	Eating out

2   Now listen again. Mark the sentences true (T) or false (F).

1   There are no changes to the history section. _____

2   They need to buy maps for the book. _____

3   The maps in the book need updating. _____

4   The opening times of the museums are the same as before. _____

5   Some new music shops will be in the book. _____

6   There are two new shopping centres. _____

7   There are some new international restaurants to include. _____

8   Charles is going back to Lahore next Friday to check the restaurants. _____

Speaking

1   What projects are you working on at the moment? Make a list of the different tasks included in a project. Which tasks have you finished? Which tasks are not ready yet? Tell your teacher about them.

2   Look at this page, unit 16, or the contents page of *Business one:one* on page 3. Discuss with your teacher which sections you have already done, which parts you have not done yet, and which ones you are still working on.

Writing

1   Write an email to your boss to update them on the project you are working on in **Speaking 1**.

2   You are visiting a city on business. Write a postcard back home, telling your family / colleagues what you have seen and done already, and what you have not done yet.

meetings

16.2

3 Now listen to the second part of the meeting. Gavin and Charles are discussing a special section on kite-flying. Read the features below, and then listen and tick (✓) which ones they will include.

Features of kite-flying	Include this?
the history of the sport	
photographs	
festivals	
how to play	
where to buy books about it	
where to buy kites	
how to make kites	

4 Put the words from the first dialogue in the correct order. Listen again to check the answers.

1 section / go / let's / each / through.
2 shall / where / start / we?
3 I / you / the copies / have / you / got / sent?
4 how to get there / add / details / got / to / still / about / I've.
5 yet / haven't / done / I / that.
6 at / the / do / weekend / I'll / it.
7 final checks / is doing / for / me / Louise / some.
8 by next Friday / get back to me / she said / she'd.

Language box

When giving updated information on a project or job, use the present perfect to explain which tasks are complete, and which are incomplete (*have* + past participle):

I've (= I have) **checked** all today's invoices.
I've done the first part of the report.
We **haven't** (= have not) sent the order yet.
He's (= he has) **already written** the letter.

In questions, notice the word order. The verb *have* is not contracted:

Have you finished the guest list?
Has the delivery arrived yet?

Look

Look again at listening scripts 16.1 and 16.2 on pages 118–119. Find more examples of the present perfect.

How to **give people news**

17

In this lesson you will learn language for giving good and bad news.

Starter

1 Do you use bathroom products with these ingredients? Match the pictures with their names.

olive (oil)   mint   lavender
almond   aloe

Expressions

1 Judith is the Director of Provence Ltd, a company which imports luxury toiletries. She has just received news about a new contract and sends this email to her colleagues.

1 What three items of news does she mention?

2 How does she want to follow up this email?

Dear All,

I'm delighted to tell you that I've just had a call from Whittaker's on Piccadilly. We've won that contract! They want to use our soaps in their Christmas bathroom hampers.
They also want us to arrange a display of soaps and creams for a private event next week on Friday. They expect fifty guests. They'd like the lavender range, and two others. Please check stocks of aloe and olive oil. Please see what samples of the creams we've got for giveaways. Let's meet on Monday to discuss.
Have a good weekend.

Judith

PS I'm afraid I'll be in France end of next week.

Speaking

1 You are chairing a staff meeting tomorrow. You will update your staff on recent and upcoming company events.

- New ID card scheme starts 1st September
- Sales figures up by 12%
- Alex Kirov is retiring – party and drinks Friday 6pm

Make notes and then practise the meeting with your teacher.

2 What has happened in the news this week? Make a note of three to four news items. Tell your teacher about each item.

Example: Sweden has won the European Cup!

Slovenia has elected a new president.

Writing

1 Write an email to all staff to summarize what you talked about at the meeting in **Speaking 1**.

2 Complete the sentences from the news items with the verbs below. Put the verb in the correct form.

arrive   announce   crash   start

1 A train _____ in the mountains.

2 The EU _____ talks on renewable energy.

3 The prime minister of Japan _____ in Paris on a state visit to France.

4 Trigbee UK, suppliers of kitchens, _____ increased profits of 15%.

meetings

Hint

samples – small amounts of something that can be tried to see what it is like
They're giving away free shampoo samples.
stock – goods that a business has for sale at any one time: **in stock / out of stock**
I'm afraid we're out of stock at the moment.
range – a set of products of a particular type, **the lavender range, a range of hand creams**

17.1

2 Judith's team meet on Monday afternoon. Although this is good news, there are some difficulties. Listen to the meeting. Mark the following sentences true (T) or false (F).

1 There are not enough sample creams to give away. _____

2 They do not have enough lavender in stock. _____

3 There are some supplies of aloe and mint soaps. _____

4 Sue cannot go to the event next week. _____

5 They cannot get supplies of almond soaps for the hampers by September. _____

6 Whittaker's will also sell the full range of soaps and creams in their shop. _____

3 Match 1–6 with a–f. Then listen again to check your answers.

1	I'm afraid	a	let you down.
2	I'm sorry	b	we have enough samples.
3	As long as	c	about that.
4	Unfortunately, I	d	is that …
5	Sorry to	e	can't.
6	The best news	f	there's a problem with …

Language box

To give news and talk about very recent events, use the present perfect, *have* + past participle.

We've **signed** a contract with a new business.

We **haven't started** the meeting yet.

This form is also used to announce the beginning of news on radio and TV.

The price of oil **has dropped** by 0.5%.

To emphasize that something happened very recently, use *just* with the present perfect:

Tom **has just arrived**. (= only a few minutes ago)

I've **just seen** him.

Look

Look again at the email in Expressions and listening script 17.1 on page 119. Find more examples of the present perfect.

Lesson record

3 new words from this lesson

1 ....
2 ....
3 ....

3 useful phrases from this lesson

1 ....
2 ....
3 ....

Things to remember

....
....
....
....
....
....

How to **make arrangements**

18

In this lesson you will learn language for making and confirming plans.

Starter

1   Have you ever been to a team-building event? Look at the following ideas for team-building activities. Which idea is best for your company?
    • camping trip
    • a day of problem-solving
    • a day of sports
    • visiting a place of historical interest

2   What events do your staff take part in to work together better?

Expressions

1   Tom O'Reilly works for Creola, an international database systems provider. He is based in Bratislava, Slovakia, and is organizing a team-building weekend in the Tatra mountains. Read the email from Tom to his assistant. He wants her to do four things. What are they?

Subject: Team-building weekend

Dear Alena,

It's not long till our trip to the High Tatras! We've booked the hotel, but please contact them to confirm it – check numbers with our staff first. Don't forget to check with Marek about transport. And another thing – it would be good to get some fresh air in the mountains. Fingers crossed for good weather! Can the hotel organize a half-day trip on the Saturday afternoon, then somewhere for dinner? (I've read about a cable car up the mountain.) Please find out.

Many thanks,

Tom

Speaking

1   You are Alena. Look at your 'to do' list, and update Tom on what you have done, and what you still need to do.

> TO DO:
> Sat trip – Cable car ✓ €20 p/p
> Fri eve – Koliba ✓ booked
> Marek ✓ 15-seater minibus, dep 15.00
> Send schedule to trainers
> Updated schedule to staff ✓ sent

Writing

1   Unfortunately, Tom is out. Write him an email with the information from **Speaking**.

2   One of your staff is celebrating twenty-five years at the company. You want to arrange a party. Email your assistant to do this. Think about venue / office room, date and time, food, drink, and a present. Add your own suggestions too. Use phrases from the emails in **Expressions** to help.

meetings

2 Read Alena's reply to Tom. The hotel offers three choices for an outing. Which is your preference? Why? What other answers does Alena have for Tom?

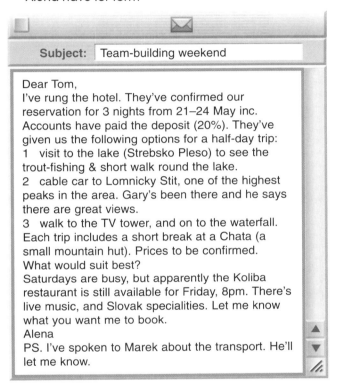

Subject: Team-building weekend

Dear Tom,
I've rung the hotel. They've confirmed our reservation for 3 nights from 21–24 May inc. Accounts have paid the deposit (20%). They've given us the following options for a half-day trip:
1 visit to the lake (Strebsko Pleso) to see the trout-fishing & short walk round the lake.
2 cable car to Lomnicky Stit, one of the highest peaks in the area. Gary's been there and he says there are great views.
3 walk to the TV tower, and on to the waterfall.
Each trip includes a short break at a Chata (a small mountain hut). Prices to be confirmed. What would suit best?
Saturdays are busy, but apparently the Koliba restaurant is still available for Friday, 8pm. There's live music, and Slovak specialities. Let me know what you want me to book.
Alena
PS. I've spoken to Marek about the transport. He'll let me know.

3 Find phrases in the emails which you can use to say the following:

1 to list a number of choices

2 to ask for a decision on number of possibilities

3 I'd like to know / please ask

4 our booking is now fixed

5 there is (free) space at the moment

6 they say / It is said (but I don't know)

7 I'm waiting for a final price / final information

8 there is something else (I want to say)

9 he will tell me when he knows.

Language box

We often use the present perfect to confirm arrangements. A lot of common verbs are irregular, and so it is important to know the past participle form.

I've told Andy to send it as soon as possible.

Have you spoken to Emma yet?

They **haven't given** me the dates.

Some irregular verbs can be grouped to help remember their past participle endings.

write, drive, choose	written / driven / chosen
find, make	found / made
send, lend	sent, lent

Look

Look again at the emails in **Expressions**. Find more examples of the present perfect.

How to **discuss options**

In this lesson you will learn language for talking about different options.

Starter

1 The following people usually wear a uniform. Can you add any more uniformed jobs to the list?

bus drivers   the police
hotel staff   factory workers

Which of these people have you seen already today / this week?

2 Match the pictures of clothes in **Expressions** with the words below.

trousers   shirt   cuff
short sleeves   turn-ups   pockets
cargo pockets   buttons   zips
belt-loops

Expressions

1 Pat works in Human Resources for an international arts centre. Her security staff need new uniforms. Pat chooses the following options for uniforms. Which do you prefer?

5 Security clothing

A   C   E

B   D   F

Speaking

1 Imagine you are in Pat's security team, but you could not go the meeting. Discuss with Pat (your teacher) some of the clothes. What features do you like / not like about them?

2 What are the advantages and disadvantages of wearing a uniform?

Language box

If you want to talk about quantity, you can use *not enough* + noun, or *too much / many* + noun.

> I **haven't got enough** time to do this. I'll do it tomorrow.

> There **aren't enough** chairs. I'll get some from Anna's office.

Much is used with uncountable nouns, *many* with countable nouns.

> Please be quiet. There's **too much** noise in here. (noise = uncountable noun)

> There are **too many** people. We need a bigger room. (people = countable noun)

meetings

Hint

You can use **exactly** to get a more specific answer to a question.

What exactly do you mean?
Where exactly are your offices?
When exactly does he arrive?

19.1 ○ **2** Listen to the meeting. Which items does Pat like best (P)? Which ones do the security staff (S) like best? Indicate below.

shirts		trousers		jackets	
a	b	c	d	e	f

3 Complete the sentences with the correct word. Listen again to check your answers.

1 I'd __opr__ for new uniforms.

2 We _____ that the blue shirt looked best.

3 Actually, I _____ the white one.

4 Let's try to make a _____ about the trousers.

5 Yes, I'd _____ those too.

6 My _____ is for the navy blue one with the zip.

7 But then maybe we'll have too much _____.

8 There aren't really enough _____ here.

Writing

Family Fun
The Cave, London SE1
Sundays @11am

family fun
fun art
sundays at 11am

drawing   music
dance   painting
      theatre

1 You work at the international arts centre, and have received an email from the marketing department asking for your opinion about two possible posters to advertise a new series of events. Write an email in reply, commenting on the features of the two posters. Consider the following points:

- size
- colours
- specific features highlighted
- typeface / font
- slogan
- background.

For emphasis, you can use *far too* + adjective / noun.

I'm sorry, but the report's **far too long**. Please cut it.

We have **far too many** applicants. We can't interview all of them.

You can also use *not ... enough* with an adjective. Notice the word order:

He's **not tall enough**. (*not* + adjective + *enough*)

It **isn't loud enough**. I can't hear you.

Look

Look again at listening script 19.1 on page 119. Find more examples of *too, enough, much,* and *many*.

Lesson record

3 new words from this lesson	3 useful phrases from this lesson
1	**1** ....
2	**2** ....
3	**3** ....

Things to remember

....
....
....
....
....
....
....

How to **give opinions**

20

In this lesson you will learn language for giving opinions, agreeing, and disagreeing.

Starter

1   Which of these things help you decide where to go on holiday?

- food and restaurants
- local transport
- museums, galleries
- nature, beaches, and wildlife
- children's activities, sports
- the weather

2   Which of these things help you decide where to choose a place for a conference?

Expressions

20.1 **1**   SpeediWings is a budget airline. In May they start weekly flights to Dubrovnik, Croatia. Robert and his colleagues are discussing an email advertisement. What two changes do they suggest?

20.2 **2**   Now listen to a later part of the meeting. How do they change the advertisement?

3   Correct the sentences from the meeting. Listen again to check your answers.

1   Well, the more important thing is to show what Dubrovnik's like.
2   Yes, definitely. I shouldn't agree more.
3   I do think it's a good idea at all.
4   You've got to point there.
5   I've not sure about that one either.
6   About these links. My feel is that three is enough.
7   Really? I'm happy I don't really agree.
8   You can be serious!

4   Look again at sentences 1–8 in **3**. Which sentences:

a   are used to give an opinion?
b   are used to agree?
c   are used to disagree?

Speaking

1   Discuss the following statements with your teacher. What do you think? Use the words in brackets to help you.

1   Budget airlines are not good for business travel. (comfort, food / drink, times, airport location, …)
2   Budget airlines are ideal for family holidays. (times, price, destinations, …)
3   On business trips there is no time for sightseeing, so the place is not important.
4   It is more relaxing to go back to the same places you know on holiday, and not explore a new country or city.

Language box

Some adjectives have two forms, -*ed*, and -*ing* endings. We use the -*ed* form to talk about how people feel:

I am **bored** with the same adverts.
We were **excited** about the new destination.

We use the -*ing* form to describe what causes the feeling:

The adverts are usually very **boring**.
The new destination is **exciting**.

Other similar adjective pairs include *interested – interesting, fascinated – fascinating, shocked – shocking.*

meetings

Hint

With a negative opinion, put **think** in the negative, and the idea in the positive:
I don't think it's a good idea to use email shots.

SpeediWings.com

Dubrovnik
New destination – book now!

Check out our routes for this summer from **Copenhagen** and **Stockholm**!

New flights weekly to **Dubrovnik**.

Book 1–30 April
Travel 1 May–30 June
From €39 one way incl tax!
SpeediWings destinations
SpeediWings timetables
Book now!

Extras?
Just a click away: Villas
Hotels
Holiday insurance
Airport transfer

Writing

1 Your company wants to start using more email advertising, sending company product news to contacts on the mailing lists. You made the following notes during a meeting about this. Now write an email to the marketing department giving your opinion.

Advantages	Disadvantages
– cheap	– impersonal, no human contact
– up-to-date mailing list	– no opportunity to talk to the receiver
– easy	– some people delete, don't read
– can send to hundreds at the same time	– people hate spam so can give a bad feeling
– so quick, can send weekly mailshots	

The *-ed* forms take a specific preposition.

bored with
excited about
fascinated by
interested in
shocked at

He is **fascinated by** the history of the old city.

I was **interested in** his trip to South America.

They were **shocked at** the number of people who booked online.

Look

Look again at listening scripts 20.1 and 20.2 on pages 119–120. Find more examples of adjectives with *-ed* and *-ing*.

How to **start and end a conversation**

21

In this lesson you will learn language for starting and ending telephone conversations.

Starter

1   Look at the pictures of a woman trying to get through to a graphic designer. Put the pictures in the correct order.

2   How often do you have problems getting through to people?

Expressions

 21.1

1   Find five mistakes in the dialogues in **Starter**.

2   Listen to check your answers.

3   Learn Elaine's part in each of the dialogues. Close your book and role-play the conversations with your teacher.

 21.2

4   Listen to the end of the conversation and answer the questions.

1   When does Harriet have to finish the flyer?

2   What is Elaine going to do next?

a
Hello, are you Harriet?

Yes, it is. Who calls please?

b
I am Elaine from Club Deluxe, Brussels.

Hello Elaine. Good to hear from you.

c
Hello, I like speak to Harriet, please.

This is Accounts. Harriet works in Design. Hold on a second.

d
Good morning. Can I speak to Harriet, please?

Yes, I put you through to Design.

Speaking

1   Role-play the following situations using the language from **Expressions**.

1   You want to ask Hans Merschoff to design some new software for your accounts department by the end of March. First ask the receptionist for Hans, and then tell Hans what you want to talk about. Finally end the conversation, saying you will send him the specifications by email.

2   First, you are a receptionist, and you put through a call from your teacher to Kioko Younie. Then, you are Kioko Younie. Talk to your teacher about a poster you have said you will design. Arrange to call your teacher back at the end of the week with your ideas.

Language box

Some verbs are often followed by another verb. In some cases we use the infinitive with *to* after the first verb:

They'd **like to have** an answer by tomorrow.

I **want to speak** to the manager!

We **forgot to send** you a new bill.

After modal verbs, like *can* and *should*, and after *will*, we use the infinitive without *to*. Modal verbs are auxiliary verbs which indicate a function like permission, possibility, or ability.

He **can't get through** to his colleague.

You **should receive** the document by tomorrow.

I'll **get back** to you by the end of the week.

5 Complete the sentences with the words used for ending a phone conversation.

1 Fine. I'll send you an email _____, then.

2 Thanks for _____.

3 Don't forget to call me if you've _____ about my email.

4 Right. We'll speak _____ then.

5 OK. I'll call you _____ 5.00.

6 Match each of the phrasal verbs *put through*, *get through*, and *hold on* with its definition.

1 _____ to wait on the phone

2 _____ to reach someone by phone

3 _____ to connect one person to another

Writing

1 You are Elaine and you have the same problem getting through to Harriet another day. Complete the email to Harriet explaining what happens every time you try to call her. Use as many modal verbs and phrasal verbs from **Expressions** and the **Language box** as you can.

Hi there Harriet,

I seem to have a problem trying to get through to you on the phone. Every time I ask for you ...

I just thought you should know about this.

Regards
Elaine

After *have to* and *be able to* we use the infinitive without *to*:
She **has to finish** the project by Friday.
We **weren't able to contact** you yesterday.

Look

Look again at listening scripts 21.1 and 21.2 on page 120. Find more examples of verbs followed by the infinitive with *to*, and modal verbs followed by the infinitive without *to*.

How to **leave a voicemail message**

In this lesson you will learn language for leaving a voicemail message.

Starter

1 How can these things make you late?

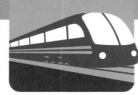

2 Are you ever late? Why?

Expressions

22.1

1 Ellis Harper is having a meeting at 12.30. He is not in his office. Listen to the messages on his voicemail and answer the questions.

1 What time is it?
2 Why is the speaker late?
3 Is it necessary to return the call?

Speaker	Time	Reason	Return the call?
1			
2			
3			

2 Now listen again. Which message are these expressions in?

Message	Expression
☐	I'm calling to see if …
☐	Hi Ellis, John here.
☐	Hopefully, I'll speak to you in a moment.
☐	Just so you know …
☐	Bye for now.
☐	Ellis, it's Rose.
☐	See you in a bit.
☐	Just to tell you …
☐	Hello Ellis, this is Sam.

Speaking

1 You are Ellis Harper returning Sam's call in **Expressions**. Sam does not answer his phone so leave him a voicemail message. Tell Sam there are usually some parking spaces in the street behind your office. Make a comment about everybody being late for the meeting. Finish the message.

Language box

Some verbs, called stative verbs, cannot be used in the present continuous when we refer to actions happening at the moment of speaking. Some stative verbs relate to feelings or emotions, e.g. *hate, love, like,* and *want*:

How **do** you **like** your new job?

It's Monday and I **don't want** to go to work.

Other stative verbs relate to mental activity, e.g. *know, mean, understand,* and *remember*.

She **understands** the problem and she's dealing with it right now.

I **don't mean** to be rude, but I don't remember your name.

Hint

We use the twenty-four-hour clock to talk about timetables.
The plane leaves at 14.45.
We pronounce **16.00** as **sixteen hundred hours.**
In normal conversation we can also use digital time, but we do not usually use the twenty-four-hour clock.

3 Write the expressions from **2** under the correct heading below.

To start the voicemail message
1
2
3

To say the reason for calling
1
2
3

To finish the voicemail message
1
2
3

"I think I'm going to be late"

Writing

1 Read the following note from a colleague. How is it different from a more formal letter?

> Hi Ahmed,
>
> Will be late tomorrow cos have doctor's appointment at 9.30 am. Should be here by 10.30, but if not can you get documents ready for meeting at 11?
> Thanks
>
> Chris

2 Think of a reason for being late for work tomorrow. Write a short note to your colleague to explain. Ask them to do something for you while you are away.

The verbs *have* and *think* are stative verbs which can also be used in the present continuous, depending on their meaning.

My boss **has** a really good idea for the new campaign.

Mireia is **having** coffee right now.

I **don't think** we're going to finish the report on time.

They**'re** happy because they**'re thinking** about the holidays.

Look

Look at listening script 22.1 on page 120. Find more examples of stative verbs.

Lesson record

3 new words from this lesson	3 useful phrases from this lesson
1	1 ....
2	2 ....
3	3 ....

Things to remember

....
....
....
....
....
....

How to **deal with telephone problems**

2 3

In this lesson you will learn language for difficult situations on the telephone.

Starter

1   What telephone problems does the receptionist in the picture have?

I'm sorry, can you speak more slowly, please?

Can you repeat your name, please?

I'm afraid I can't hear you at all.

I'm afraid Olympia Patel doesn't work here.

Mr Cybulska? Are you there? Mr Cybulska?

Please excuse me a moment.

Expressions

23.1

1   Listen to Kiko take a difficult call. What problems does she have? Does she deal with the problems well?

2   Complete the sentences with words for dealing with problems on the telephone.

1   I'm sorry, who's _____? Can you repeat _____ , please?

2   I'm _____ , I still didn't _____ your name. Could you _____ it again, please?

3   _____ me a _____ . I've got another _____ .

4   Sorry _____ that. What can I _____ for you?

5   I'm _____ I can't hear you.

6   I think we got _____ .

7   Thanks. I'll _____ you straight _____ .

Speaking

1   You work with the following people:

Paula	David	Karen
Thoma	Alan	Maria.

Your teacher will call each of your colleagues in turn. Answer your teacher depending on the number you throw on the dice.

1   The caller says something you cannot understand. (Continue the dialogue)

2   It is a wrong number. (The call finishes)

3   You do not recognize the caller. (Continue the dialogue)

4   You are cut off. (The call finishes)

5   Your phone rings with another call. (Continue the dialogue)

6   You connect the caller to someone else in your office. (The call finishes)

telephoning

Hint

When we try to fix a problem, but the problem continues, we use **still**. **Still** shows that there is no change in the problem.
The computer's not working. I'll just change the cable. No, it's still not working.

3 Look at the telephone dialogues. Correct the receptionist's rude responses.

1 **Caller** I'd like to speak to Matti, please.
Receptionist There's no Matti here.

2 **Caller** Ich möchte bitte mit Claudia sprechen.
Receptionist What?

3 **Caller** Oh hello. It's Mehmet here.
Receptionist Who?

4 **Caller** It's about the project.
Receptionist Wait. I have to answer the other phone.

5 **Caller** Hello, it's Mehmet again. We were speaking a minute ago.
Receptionist What happened to you?

6 **Caller** I wanted to talk to Stuart about the JW111.
Receptionist I don't know what you're saying.

23.2 ○ **4** Now listen to check your answers.

Writing

1 Look at the note below. What does Luc ask Sara to do?

Hi Sara,

Sorry, but I'm not going to be in the office tomorrow.
Could you answer my telephone for me, please?
Thanks a lot. See you on Wednesday.

Luc

2 Imagine that you are not going to be in your office tomorrow. Write a note to a colleague to ask them to do something for you.

Look

Look again at listening script 23.1 on page 120. Find more examples of *can* and *could* for requests. There is one other use of *can* in the listening script. What is it?

Language box

When we ask for something, we often use the construction *Can I have ...*

Can I have your name, please?

Can I have a contact number, please?

If we want to sound slightly more polite, we can use the form *could*:

Could I have your bank details, please?

Could I have an email address, please?

We also use *can* and *could* to ask someone to do something for us:

Can you speak more slowly, please?

Could you repeat that, please?

We use *can* when offering to help other people:

Can I get you anything?

Lesson record

3 new words from this lesson	3 useful phrases from this lesson
1	1 ....
2	2 ....
3	3 ....

Things to remember

....
....
....
....
....
....

How to **make a follow-up call**

24

In this lesson you will learn language for commenting on a previous call.

Starter

1 Look at these ideas for celebrating the tenth anniversary of your company. What are the three different options? Which one would you choose? Why?

Animalia
Nature Theme Park

Presents the ultimate experience!

Welcome drinks in the tropical jungle house.

Tour of the different ecosystems complete with dolphin show.

Dinner in the Oasis Restaurant.

A party with a difference.

€120 a head.

---

exclusive restaurant for your company celebrations

delicious five-course meal accompanied by a superb selection of the best wines

live entertainment by Comedy & Co. Incorporated

to follow, champagne, chocolates, and chill-out music

€150 a head

the artichokeheart

Top-class nightclub offers non-stop excitement.

Live music by top bands.

Free drinks from start to finish.

Celebrity guests making surprise appearances.

The night of your life!

€100 a head

Sight & Sound

---

telephoning

Speaking

1 Choose one of the other events in **Starter**. You have already telephoned the place once to find out about the price and the main attractions. Think of three follow-up questions about:
   - food / drink
   - entertainment
   - price

2 Role-play a telephone conversation with your teacher and ask your three questions. You are the person organizing the celebration, and your teacher works for the venue you choose.

Hint

These three-syllable words are stressed on the first syllable: **popular**, **interested**, **comfortable**.

These three-syllable words are stressed on the second syllable: **delicious**, **expensive**, **exotic**.

Expressions

24.1

1 Anne Kechel wants to book Animalia for her company party. She spoke to Gerda Honne at Animalia once before, and is now making a follow-up call to ask for more information. Listen and answer the questions.

1 When did Anne and Gerda last speak?

2 What extra information does Anne ask for?

2 Complete the sentences with the words used for making a follow-up call.

1 We were _____ last week about _____ our anniversary party in Animalia.

2 I wanted to _____ you a few _____ before we make our final _____ .

3 Well, you _____ a tour of the park when we _____ .

4 Only we _____ think about this _____ week.

5 The price you _____ me is _____ person.

6 I'll _____ back to you next week _____ our decision, OK?

Writing

1 Read the email Gerda sends Anne. Which words are used to refer to topics from their telephone conversation?

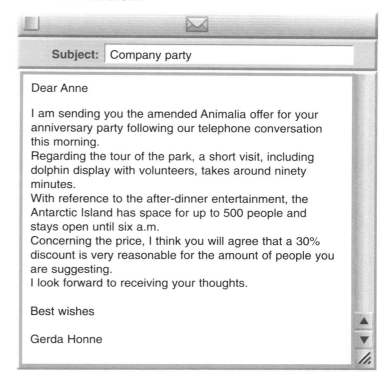

Subject: Company party

Dear Anne

I am sending you the amended Animalia offer for your anniversary party following our telephone conversation this morning.
Regarding the tour of the park, a short visit, including dolphin display with volunteers, takes around ninety minutes.
With reference to the after-dinner entertainment, the Antarctic Island has space for up to 500 people and stays open until six a.m.
Concerning the price, I think you will agree that a 30% discount is very reasonable for the amount of people you are suggesting.
I look forward to receiving your thoughts.

Best wishes

Gerda Honne

2 Write a similar email based on your role-play in **Speaking**.

Language box

We use *really*, *very*, or *extremely* to make an adjective stronger:

The contract is **extremely important**.

The scenery is **very attractive**.

This book is **really interesting**.

We use *a bit* to make the adjective weaker:

The restaurant is **a bit small** for us.

We often use *a bit* when we are not happy about something:

Your music is **a bit loud**. Can you turn it down?

Look

Look again at listening script 24.1 on page 121. Find more examples of *really*, *very*, *extremely*, and *a bit*.

Lesson record

3 new words from this lesson

1 ....
2 ....
3 ....

3 useful phrases from this lesson

1 ....
2 ....
3 ....

Things to remember

....
....
....
....
....
....

How to **take and leave messages**

25

In this lesson you will learn language for dealing with telephone messages.

Starter

1 Look at the reasons why people may not be able to answer a phone call. Complete each one with one of the prepositions below.

on   at   on   at   in   off

1 They are _____ another line.

2 They are _____ holiday.

3 They are not _____ their desk.

4 They are _____ sick.

5 They are _____ a meeting.

6 They are _____ lunch.

2 What do you usually do: leave a message or call back later?

Expressions

25.1 ○ 1 Listen to four short telephone conversations and answer the questions for each dialogue.

1 Why can't the caller speak to the person they are calling?

2 What does the caller do: leave a message or say they will call back later?

2 Now listen again. Complete the sentences with the words used for taking and leaving messages.

1 Can I _____ a message?

2 Could you ask him to _____ me back, please?

3 Can you _____ him a message for me, then?

4 Could you _____ him I called and ask him ...?

5 Shall I _____ her a message?

6 Who shall I _____ called?

Speaking

1 Look at the messages and role-play the phone conversations. In each case you have to leave a message. Your teacher answers the phone.

Message for: Oscar Kinsley
Time: 11.25
Caller: Jürgen Richter
Company: RDK Transport Services

Message: Problem with delivery.
Wants you to call back.

Tel. no.: 0049 835 30925

Message for: Rose Lahiri
Time: 15.50
Caller: Linda Chong
Company: International Motor Group

Message: Called about March bill.
Wants you to send copy.

Tel. no.: 0086 9371 2860

telephoning

Hint

We can say **fifteen minutes** or **quarter of an hour**. Similarly, thirty minutes is **half an hour**, forty-five minutes is **three quarters of an hour**, and **ninety minutes** is **an hour and a half**.

3 Have you ever forgotten to pass on a message? What happened?

4 Find six mistakes in the dialogue.

> Erin   Could I speak to Yann, please?
>
> **Receptionist   I'm afraid he's on a meeting right now. I gave him a message?**
>
> Erin   Yes, please. It's really important he gets it.
>
> **Receptionist   Don't worry. I'll pass it on as soon as he finishes. Who I say called?**
>
> Erin   This is Erin McCabe from Head Office. Can you tell to him that the meeting on Friday in Brussels has been cancelled?
>
> **Receptionist   Brussels meeting Friday cancelled ...**
>
> Erin   Can you ask him to call back me as soon as possible?
>
> **Receptionist   No problem. Do you give me a contact number?**

Writing

1 We often omit words when writing messages. Look at the messages in **Speaking**. Which words are omitted?

2 Write a message for conversations **1**, **2**, and **4** in listening script 25.1, omitting the words which are not necessary.

"I'M AFRAID THEY'RE ALL IN A MEETING..."

Look

Look again at listening script 25.1 on page 121. Find more examples of *ask* and *tell* for leaving messages.

Language box

We often use *ask* and *tell* when we leave a message for somebody. We use *ask* with questions:

> Can you **ask** her if she got my email?
> Could you **ask** him when he wants the report?

We *tell* somebody information:

> **Tell** him (that) I can't come to the meeting on Friday.
> She **told** me (that) she was ill.

When we want somebody to do something, we use *ask* + person + infinitive:

> Please **ask him to send** me a fax.

We can also use *tell* + person + infinitive:

> Can you **tell her to call** me in the morning?

Lesson record

3 new words from this lesson	3 useful phrases from this lesson
1	**1** ....
2	**2** ....
3	**3** ....

Things to remember

....
....
....
....
....
....

How to **use a mobile phone**

In this lesson you will learn language for answering a mobile phone.

Starter

1 Look at the pictures and write down where the person is.

2 Do you answer your mobile phone in these situations? Why / Why not?

Expressions

1 You are going to hear six people answer their mobile phones. Complete the table.

	Where are they?	Can they speak?
1		
2		
3		
4		
5		
6		

Speaking

1 Role-play a conversation with your teacher for each of the situations in **Starter**. When your teacher calls, roll a dice and look at the number below to find out how to respond.

1 polite – can't talk
2 informal – can't talk
3 informal – can talk
4 polite – can talk
5 informal – can't talk
6 you choose how to answer

telephoning

26.2 **2** Now listen to two more responses. Are they more or less formal than those in **1**?

3 Put the phrases in the correct column in the table below.

a Call me back in an hour, OK?

b No, I've got plenty of time.

c No, you're not disturbing me.

d I'll call you right back.

e No, it's all right. I don't mind.

f Can't talk right now.

g Would you mind calling me back this afternoon?

h How can I help you?

When you can speak	When you can't speak

Writing

1 Look at the text message your colleague has sent you. Do you understand it?

2 Are the following necessary or unnecessary in a text message?

• correct spelling

• complete words

• pronouns

• punctuation

• opening and closing expressions

3 Write a text message of your own to reply to David. Explain you are in a taxi, because your car has broken down, and you will be about ten minutes late.

Look

Look again at listening scripts 26.1 and 26.2 on page 121. Find more examples of present continuous with *at the moment* and *just*.

Language box

We use the present continuous to talk about actions that are happening at the same time as we are speaking:

Who's Imelda talking to?

They're discussing the budget for next year.

When we want to emphasize the time that we are referring to, we can use the expressions *right now* and *at the moment*:

He's leaving the office right now.

What are you doing at the moment?

We can also use the adverb *just*:

I'm just getting into the lift.

We're just coming through the door.

Lesson record

3 new words from this lesson	3 useful phrases from this lesson
1	1 ....
2	2 ....
3	3 ....

Things to remember

....

....

....

....

....

Telephone overview

27

In this lesson you will revise and practise the telephone expressions from lessons 21 to 26.

Starter

1 Which is the most difficult thing for you to do on the telephone in English? Put the following in order: 1 = the most difficult, 8 = the easiest.

_____ answering a mobile phone when you are busy

_____ starting a conversation

_____ leaving a voicemail message

_____ dealing with problems on the phone

_____ making a follow-up call

_____ taking a message

_____ ending a conversation

_____ leaving a message

2 Tell your teacher about a difficult phone call you have made.

Instructions

1 You will need a dice to play the game. The object is to win a line of four squares by throwing the dice and role-playing the conversations. Look at the instructions and play the game with your teacher.

1 You start. Throw the dice and look at the square with the same number. Do the role-play. Your teacher responds, where necessary. Then write your initials on that square to show you have won it.

2 Now your teacher throws the dice and repeats the process. If the square already belongs to one player, it is not necessary to role-play the conversation again, and the next player throws the dice.

3 If a player gets a six, they can choose a bonus square. They start the role-play as usual.

4 Continue until one player has four squares in a line, or all the squares have been won. If neither player has a line of four, the winner is the player with the most squares.

Practice

1 Match 1–10 with a–j to make complete sentences.

1	No, I'm a bit busy.	a from Associated Fashion Lines.
2	Speaking. Who's	b 01 5443 00876.
3	OK. I'll call	c ask you some questions first.
4	Great. That'll	d about a booking in February.
5	Yes, it's Chris Ettinger	e I'll call you back this afternoon, OK?
6	Well, actually, I wanted to	f Can you hear me now?
7	Yes, we were talking last week	g you after lunch.
8	I'm afraid he's not in the	h be good.
9	Yes, it's	i calling?
10	Is that better? I'm going outside.	j office right now. Who's calling?

 27.1 **2** Listen and choose a suitable response from the sentences above.

telephoning

Leave a message on a colleague's voicemail, checking they have received an order.	You call a wrong number. Apologize and end the call.	You call a British company, but the receptionist doesn't understand you at first. Spell your name for them.	Your colleague is having lunch. Leave a message with the receptionist to say when you'll call back.
Your colleague answers the phone, but you have a bad line. Offer to send an email.	You call a colleague, but they don't recognize you. Explain who you are.	Apologize to a caller for cutting them off.	A colleague calls you, but you're driving. Tell them when you'll call them back.
Interrupt your call to take another call. Apologize after you take it.	Accept a call on your mobile. You've got ten minutes before a conference call.	Leave a message on your colleague's voicemail, explaining why you're going to be late.	Phone a supplier. Explain that you phoned them last week about some new posters.
Ask to speak to the Human Resources manager and explain to the receptionist what you want.	Call a colleague abroad and arrange a meeting for next week for when you visit their office.	Call a client to ask if they are interested in an offer you sent them last week.	Your colleague is sick. Answer their phone and take a message from the caller.

How to make first contact

28

In this lesson you will learn language for contacting a person or company for the first time by email.

Starter

> **supplier** /səˈplaɪə(r)/ a person or company that provides goods for other companies
> **supply teacher** teacher employed

1 Put the sentences in the correct order to make an email.

a _____ Zhang Xian

b _____ My name is Zhang Xian and I am the Purchasing manager of PTK Ltd.

c _____ I would be grateful if you could send me a brochure of your products and services.

d _____ Yours faithfully

e _____ Dear Sir

f _____ I am interested in your new range of shelving.

Expressions

1 Look at these two first contacts by email and say which one you think is better, and why.

2 What is good / bad about each email? Answer the questions below.

- Is it in the right style?
- Is the greeting correct?
- Is the information complete?
- Is too much information included?
- Does the reader know what to do next?

3 Look at the emails again.

1 Find a more formal way to say:

we need _____

I think that _____

exactly what we want _____

tell us your price _____

I am from (this company) _____

send me an email _____ .

2 Find a way to end an email:

that begins *Dear Sir / Madam*

_____

a friendly but polite ending _____ .

Practice

1 Write a reply from the potential supplier to Mr Lasnier at duMidi. Try to include all the information below.

- already happy customers in Italy and Spain
- interested in new business in Europe
- an order of that size is standard
- six to eight weeks to ship via Saigon
- many different models / designs – please say exactly what you want

2 Write a first email from your company to a potential supplier.

Language box

The difference between *make* and *do*:
do is usually about actions
make is usually about producing, or constructing.

However, there are a lot of different contexts for each verb.

***Do* for indefinite activities (often with *something*, *anything*, etc.):**
Then she did something surprising.
I like doing nothing at the weekend.

***Do* for work or study:**
I'm doing a Master's in Industrial Psychology.
I'm not going to do any work this afternoon.

***Do* + *-ing*:**
We have to do a lot of thinking.
We should do some reorganizing of this office.

Hint

To say what your role in the company is, you can use **the person responsible for** + noun / gerund.
I'm the person responsible for purchasing / human resources / logistics.
Can I speak to the person responsible for technical specifications?

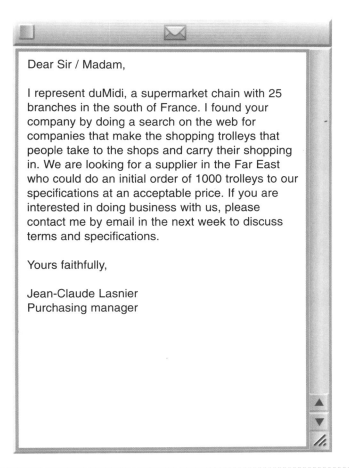

Dear Sir / Madam,

I represent duMidi, a supermarket chain with 25 branches in the south of France. I found your company by doing a search on the web for companies that make the shopping trolleys that people take to the shops and carry their shopping in. We are looking for a supplier in the Far East who could do an initial order of 1000 trolleys to our specifications at an acceptable price. If you are interested in doing business with us, please contact me by email in the next week to discuss terms and specifications.

Yours faithfully,

Jean-Claude Lasnier
Purchasing manager

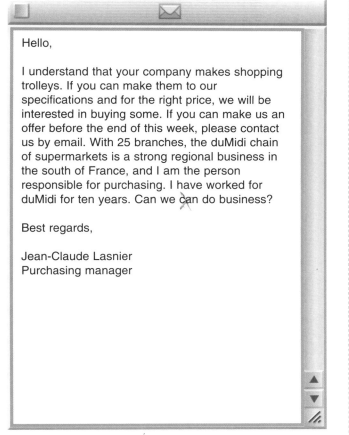

Hello,

I understand that your company makes shopping trolleys. If you can make them to our specifications and for the right price, we will be interested in buying some. If you can make us an offer before the end of this week, please contact us by email. With 25 branches, the duMidi chain of supermarkets is a strong regional business in the south of France, and I am the person responsible for purchasing. I have worked for duMidi for ten years. Can we can do business?

Best regards,

Jean-Claude Lasnier
Purchasing manager

Make for constructing, creating, or building, etc.

> Could you make a copy of this?
> Let's make a plan.

Make can be used with two objects:

> Can you make me a full business plan?

Some words that go (or collocate) with *do*:

> work   a job   business   someone a favour

Some words that go (or collocate) with *make*:

> progress   an offer   a call   arrangements

Look

Look again at the emails in **Expressions**. Find more examples of *make* and *do*. Group them under the rules in the **Language box**.

Lesson record

3 new words from this lesson	3 useful phrases from this lesson
1	1 ....
2	2 ....
3	3 ....

Things to remember

....
....
....
....
....
....

How to **get information**

In this unit you will learn language for finding out what you need to know in an email.

Starter

> **outsourcing** /ˈaʊtsɔːsɪŋ/ closing a department inside a company, and giving the department's work to another company
>
> **outspoken** /aʊtˈspəʊkən/ saying

1 Read the definition of outsourcing and look at the list of company departments below. Which ones are the most likely to be outsourced?

- Cleaning
- Finance
- Security
- Catering
- Human Resources
- IT

Expressions

Practice

1 You will be visiting Luxembourg next month, and while you are there you would also like to attend a talk by a European Commissioner. Email the Commission office in Luxembourg to try to arrange it. Find out:

- if you can bring colleagues
- if you have to pay
- if you need security papers, etc.
- where the talk is
- if you can get the information by next Wednesday.

Language box

We use indirect language to get information politely:

> We would like to know if you are interested.
>
> I would like to know your availability.
>
> Can you tell me if you have the correct software?
>
> Could you tell me if the specifications are correct?

We also use indirect language to make requests politely:

> Would it be possible to visit you next Thursday?
>
> Would it be possible for you to visit our factory?
>
> Would you be able to give us a discount?

Hint

Let (us) know is a request for information.
If you have any problems with the installation, please let me know.
Please let us know if your system has capacity for 500 units.

1 David from Highforce Training left a message at Network Solutions about outsourcing CD-ROM development. Look at the reply and put the sentences into the correct order.

To: d.owens@highforcetraining.co.uk

From: i.gupta@networksolutions.com

Dear Mr Owens,

a _____ Secondly, which software should the CD-ROMs be able to work with?

b _____ Would it be possible for you to get back to me on these questions?

c _____ Firstly, could you tell me if a specification document is available?

d _____ Thank you for your message about outsourcing your CD-ROM development.

e _____ This is definitely a project that we would be interested in.

f _____ I hope to hear from you soon.

g _____ However, we would like to have some more details, before confirming whether we could go ahead.

Yours sincerely,
Indira Gupta
Business Development Manager

2 This is the email David Owens was going to send to Indira Gupta. How could you improve it?

To: i.gupta@networksolutions.com

From: d.owens@highforcetraining.co.uk

Dear Indira,
I'm writing on behalf of Network Solutions. Are you interested in working for Highforce? Would you be able to produce one of our interactive CD-ROMs in six weeks, if you receive the complete info from us? Furthermore, can you provide the after sales service that we need (see Aftersales attachment)? Highforce are looking for a long-term business partner in India to outsource this work to and would like to know your feelings about this. Finally, we would like to receive a global price for these services from you. Would you be able to provide this, please?
I look forward to hearing from you.
David Owens
Logistics

29.1 ○ 3 David checked the email with his boss Marisa, before sending it. Listen to the dialogue and correct his email.

4 Did Marisa make the same changes as you?

We can use direct questions to get specific information:

What time will he arrive?

What is the budget for this project?

Look

Look again at the emails in **Expressions**. Find more examples of indirect language and *let us know*.

Lesson record

3 new words from this lesson

3 useful phrases from this lesson

1 ....

2 ....

3 ....

1 ....

2 ....

3 ....

Things to remember

....

....

....

....

....

....

....

How to follow something up

In this unit you will learn ways to develop a business relationship by email.

Starter

> **to follow something up** (phrasal verb) to react after receiving a piece of news or information by trying to find out more information about it

30.1

1 Put this trade fair dialogue in the correct order. Then listen and check your answers.

a _____ Thank you.

b _____ Your product looks quite interesting.

c _____ Well, please take my card and get in touch.

d _____ Would you like to see how it works?

e _____ I'm afraid I don't have time right now.

2 Which verb on the recording means:

- to make something faster? _____
- to contact somebody? _____
- to investigate more? _____

Expressions

1 Think again about the next contact between Dr Abbas and Mrs Hanhisalo in **Starter**.

   1 Who would make the next contact? Would it be by phone or by email?

   2 What are the advantages and disadvantages of phone and email?

Practice

1 Mrs Hanhisalo also wrote a follow-up email. Choose the best words to complete her email on the right.

2 Write Mrs Hanhisalo's email reply to Dr Abbas' email in **Expressions**.

3 Write an email following up a first contact you made recently at work or socially.

Dear Dr Abbas,
I would like to thank you for *visit / visiting* our stand at the Berlin trade fair last week. I enjoyed *to meet / meeting* you there and I hope that you found the fair useful. I remember that you were interested in *find / finding* out more about our new HPLC. *Would / Do* you like me to post our full brochure, including prices? I am sure that you would find this HPLC faster and more reliable than anything else that is *be / being* offered on the market at present. Naturally, installation, back-up, and training are all *included / including* in the price. If there is any more information I can help you with, please do not hesitate *to ask / asking*.
Best regards,
Dr Kirsi Hanhisalo
Development manager

email

Hint

As well as is a very common alternative to **and**. It is followed by a noun or pronoun.

Would it be possible for you to send the full technical specifications, as well as the current prices?

Dr Pavlov agreed with the idea, as well as Dr O'Neill.

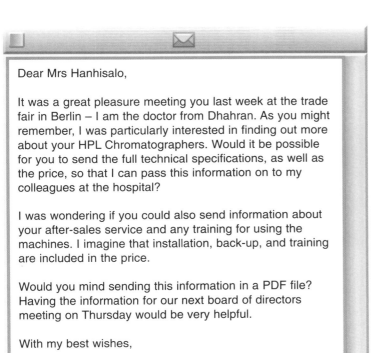

Dear Mrs Hanhisalo,

It was a great pleasure meeting you last week at the trade fair in Berlin – I am the doctor from Dhahran. As you might remember, I was particularly interested in finding out more about your HPL Chromatographers. Would it be possible for you to send the full technical specifications, as well as the price, so that I can pass this information on to my colleagues at the hospital?

I was wondering if you could also send information about your after-sales service and any training for using the machines. I imagine that installation, back-up, and training are included in the price.

Would you mind sending this information in a PDF file? Having the information for our next board of directors meeting on Thursday would be very helpful.

With my best wishes,

Dr Hassan Abbas
Head of Diagnostic Laboratory
Azizaya Hospital
PO Box 38
Dhahran 313 90
Kingdom of Saudi Arabia

2 This is the email that Dr Abbas wrote to Mrs Hanhisalo. Read the email. Mark the sentences true (T) or false (F).

1 Dr Abbas' hospital is definitely going to buy some of these machines. _____

2 Mrs Hanhisalo should send the information by courier. _____

3 The decision about buying these machines will be taken by a committee, not just one person. _____

3 What expression does Dr Abbas use to:

introduce himself?

a _____

introduce the main topic?

b _____

ask her politely to do something?

c _____

explain why he wants something?

d _____

ask her politely and indirectly to do something?

e _____

ask for a kind of computer file?

f _____

Language box

The gerund (or the *-ing* form) is very common in English. It can be used as the **subject of a sentence or a clause:**

Learning a new language is never easy.

Meeting you was a great pleasure.

As the **object of a sentence or a clause**, for example after *like, love, enjoy, mind, hate, dislike*:

She loves **getting** little surprises.

Would you mind **waiting**, sir?

After prepositions:

Is it true that you're frightened of **flying**?

We have no hope of **winning** this.

Look

Look again at Dr Abbas' email in **Expressions**. Find more examples of the gerund.

How to book or buy by email

In this lesson you will learn language for reserving and buying by email.

Starter

1   Have you ever bought or booked anything online? Tell your teacher:
  • what it was
  • the site
  • the cost
  • how you paid
  • extra money you had to pay (postage, etc.).

2   List the advantages and disadvantages of booking or buying online.

Expressions

1   A German company wants to rent new office space in Greece. Two of the staff are responsible for finding the new premises. Complete the sentences in the email on page 65 with the expressions below.
  • view the property
  • reach an agreement
  • if it is convenient
  • suit our needs

2   Mr Kuepper went to Greece and viewed the office. Afterwards, he sent another email. Choose the best words to complete the second email.

Practice

1   Mr Kuepper stayed at the Dionysios Hotel. Put the sentences (a–h) in the correct order to make his email reservation.

  a   Firstly, is breakfast included? _____

  b   I would like two single rooms with bathrooms for myself and a colleague, Uschi Lenz. _____

  c   Secondly, how much would these rooms be on those dates? _____

  d   I have two questions though. _____

  e   We would prefer quiet rooms. _____

  f   I hope to hear from you soon. _____

  g   I am writing to you to book rooms at your hotel. _____

  h   We will arrive on Monday 6th September and leave on Wednesday 8th. _____

2   Write emails with your teacher, about a process of buying or booking something. Include:
  • first email from client saying what is wanted, ask about availability and price
  • reply email from supplier answering questions and asking for more details
  • second email from client answering questions and buying / booking it
  • second email from supplier confirming the booking / order. Give extra details.

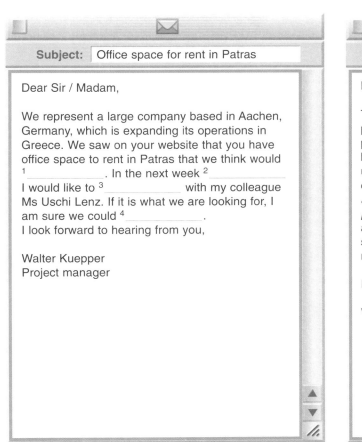

Subject: Office space for rent in Patras

Dear Sir / Madam,

We represent a large company based in Aachen, Germany, which is expanding its operations in Greece. We saw on your website that you have office space to rent in Patras that we think would
¹ _____ . In the next week ² _____
I would like to ³ _____ with my colleague Ms Uschi Lenz. If it is what we are looking for, I am sure we could ⁴ _____ .
I look forward to hearing from you,

Walter Kuepper
Project manager

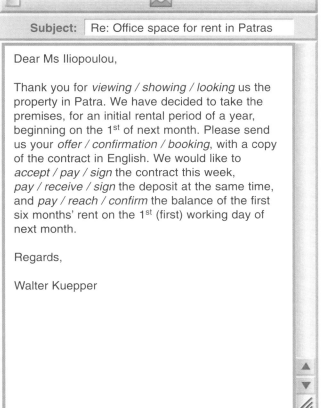

Subject: Re: Office space for rent in Patras

Dear Ms Iliopoulou,

Thank you for *viewing / showing / looking* us the property in Patra. We have decided to take the premises, for an initial rental period of a year, beginning on the 1st of next month. Please send us your *offer / confirmation / booking*, with a copy of the contract in English. We would like to *accept / pay / sign* the contract this week, *pay / receive / sign* the deposit at the same time, and *pay / reach / confirm* the balance of the first six months' rent on the 1st (first) working day of next month.

Regards,

Walter Kuepper

Language box

When two words often go together, they *collocate*. Here are some frequent collocations for buying and booking.

> You can: *confirm a booking, cancel a booking, receive confirmation of a booking.*
> You can: *view a property, develop a property, show a property.*
> You can: *make an offer, think about an offer, reject an offer, accept an offer.*
> You can: *agree on a price, agree a date.*
> You can: *pay a deposit, pay the balance.*

Look

Look again at the collocations in the **Language box**. Which ones could be used for booking something? Which ones could be used for renting or buying something?

Lesson record

3 new words from this lesson	3 useful phrases from this lesson
1	1 ....
2	2 ....
3	3 ....

Things to remember

....
....
....
....
....
....

How to complain by email

In this lesson you will learn language for complaining politely by email.

Starter

1 Look at the cartoon. What has happened?

2 Have you ever had to complain about something you bought?
   • What did you buy?
   • What did you do about it?

Expressions

1 Read the email below. Is it polite or impolite?

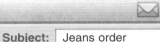

Subject: Jeans order

Dear Sir or Madam,

On the 28th of February I ordered a pair of jeans (size XS) from you. Confirmation came immediately, but when your package arrived today, it was a pair of jeans in size XXL. There seems to have been some confusion with another order. In addition, you appear to have charged me €49.99, which is not the correct price for the item I ordered. Please send the correct jeans as soon as possible. Meanwhile, what shall I do with the other pair?

Yours,

Jane Harris

Practice

1 Use the language from **Expressions** and the **Language box** to make this complaining email more polite and effective. Try to add *seem to* and *appear to* to introduce mistakes or problems.

 email

Subject: T-shirts and travel bags

Dear Mr Lee,

For our 30th annual convention, we ordered 500 travel bags with T-shirts with our company logo. You told us the order would be here one week before the convention, but it only arrived today! What's worse, the printing of the logo is upside down. On top of that, your bill is for €5,000 and that's just wrong! The correct price is €4,000. Your service is incompetent, and I demand a full replacement as soon as possible.

Yours sincerely,
Pilar Romero
Purchasing Dept.

Hint

To be polite, we often begin complaints with
I am afraid:
I am afraid there is a mistake in the invoice.

Hint

The noun form of **to complain** is **a complaint**.
Excuse me, I'd like to make a complaint.
There has been a complaint about our delivery.

2 Find expressions from the email which match the meanings below.

I bought (by email)

you said you could supply it

what caused the problem

another thing is

I think your bill is wrong

this is what I want you to do

tell me what to do

3 A group of students have done a summer course at a university. Read their email on the right. What four things do they complain about?

4 Complete the sentences in the email on the right with the words used for complaining below.

- were not of a very high standard
- a reduction of
- which we recently attended
- Please send us
- a deposit of
- which is not the correct price
- but I am afraid there is a mistake
- standard of service
- All in all

Dear Ms Hay,

We booked 25 places on the Coral University summer school Economics I course, 1_____. The bill has just arrived, 2_____ in it. You have overcharged us, because your bill is for AU $ 87,500, 3_____ for the course, because we have already paid 4_____ $ 875 per person. In addition, the course was 175 hours long, instead of 200, so there should be 5_____ 12.5%. 6_____ a corrected bill. Meanwhile, we would like you to know that the facilities 7_____. Firstly, the classrooms seemed to have no air-conditioning and they were poor quality. Secondly, they were a long way from the main campus facilities. 8_____, we are dissatisfied with the 9_____ that the university provided.

Yours sincerely,

Ya Xi

5 Look again at the emails in **1** and **4**. Do they include any exclamation marks (!)? If not, why not?

Language box

To complain, we often use the verbs *seem* and *appear*.

There **seems** to be something wrong.

You **appear** to have charged us €15,000 instead of €14,000.

Use these nouns to talk about mistakes:

I found two **mistakes** in the bill.

We think this must be an **error**.

Charged is a common verb used to talk about the wrong amount of money:

We feel that you have **charged** us too much.

Look

Look again at the emails in Expressions. Find more examples of *seem, appear, charged,* and nouns used to talk about mistakes.

Lesson record

3 new words from this lesson

1
2
3

3 useful phrases from this lesson

1
2
3

Things to remember

Email overview

33

In this lesson you will revise and practise the email expressions from lessons 28 to 32.

Starter

1 What does your office look like?

2 Are there noticeboards or pictures on the walls?

3 Do workers in your office decorate their working space in some way? How?

Instructions

1 Look at some of these emails quickly and answer the questions.
   1 Who is David Stoner?
   2 Who is Kim Ho?
   3 Why are these two people emailing each other?

2 One of the emails does not belong in the sequence. Which one? Why not?

3 Discuss the questions below with your teacher.
   1 Which of the photos 1–6 has Mr Stoner decided to buy?
   2 What expressions show that this sequence is polite but friendly?
   3 How do the emails change as the sequence progresses?
   4 In your culture, is it normal to be more direct or less direct than the two people in this sequence?

4 Tell your teacher about an email sequence you have been involved with.

5 Imagine that you are Kim Ho and your teacher is David Stoner. Role-play the negotiation with your teacher as if you were on the telephone.

1

2

3

4

5

6

email

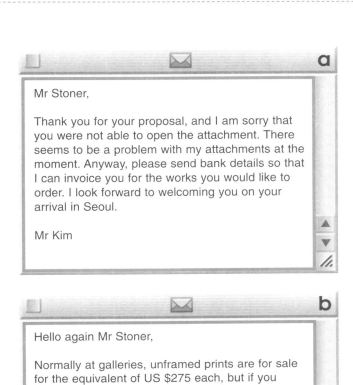

a

Mr Stoner,

Thank you for your proposal, and I am sorry that you were not able to open the attachment. There seems to be a problem with my attachments at the moment. Anyway, please send bank details so that I can invoice you for the works you would like to order. I look forward to welcoming you on your arrival in Seoul.

Mr Kim

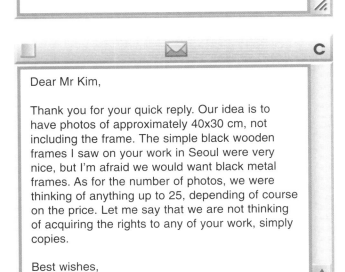

b

Hello again Mr Stoner,

Normally at galleries, unframed prints are for sale for the equivalent of US $275 each, but if you order more than 20, I could reduce the price to US $200. Would you like me to get a quote for the frames? I have attached my catalogue so that you can choose which images you would like. And please, call me Ho.

Kim Ho

c

Dear Mr Kim,

Thank you for your quick reply. Our idea is to have photos of approximately 40x30 cm, not including the frame. The simple black wooden frames I saw on your work in Seoul were very nice, but I'm afraid we would want black metal frames. As for the number of photos, we were thinking of anything up to 25, depending of course on the price. Let me say that we are not thinking of acquiring the rights to any of your work, simply copies.

Best wishes,
David Stoner

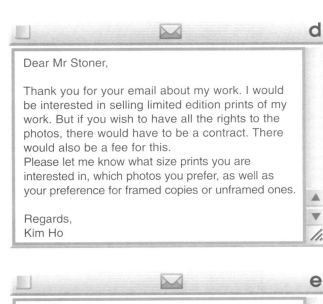

d

Dear Mr Stoner,

Thank you for your email about my work. I would be interested in selling limited edition prints of my work. But if you wish to have all the rights to the photos, there would have to be a contract. There would also be a fee for this.
Please let me know what size prints you are interested in, which photos you prefer, as well as your preference for framed copies or unframed ones.

Regards,
Kim Ho

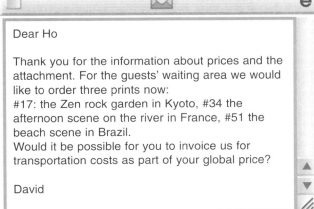

e

Dear Ho

Thank you for the information about prices and the attachment. For the guests' waiting area we would like to order three prints now:
#17: the Zen rock garden in Kyoto, #34 the afternoon scene on the river in France, #51 the beach scene in Brazil.
Would it be possible for you to invoice us for transportation costs as part of your global price?

David

f

Dear Mr Kim,

I saw an exhibition of your photographs recently while on business in Seoul. I am Project Manager of The Scargill Foundation (I have attached a link to our website),and we have recently moved into new offices. I am responsible for making the space attractive for visitors and staff. I would be very interested in purchasing some prints of your work to decorate our offices.

I look forward to hearing from you,
David Stoner
Project Manager
Scargill Foundation

How to deal with airport problems

In this lesson you will learn language to use when you land at an airport.

Starter

1 Put the phrases in the order they happen when you land at an airport.

   _1_   You get off the plane.

   _____   You collect your suitcase.

   _____   You leave the airport.

   _____   You pass through Immigration.

   _____   You go to baggage reclaim.

   _____   You enter the arrivals hall.

   _____   You pass through Customs.

   _____   You find a trolley.

2 When was the last time you arrived at an airport? Tell your teacher what you did when you landed.

Expressions

1 Use the words from **Starter** to describe the pictures a–d.

a

b

c

d

34.1

2 Danilo arrives at Tokyo Narita International Airport. Listen to the two conversations and answer the questions.

   1   Where exactly in the airport is he?

   2   What problems does he have?

Speaking

1 Role-play the following situations using the language from the unit.

   1   You arrive at Bangkok International Airport for a business meeting. Unfortunately, your luggage does not arrive in baggage reclaim, and you cannot see any taxis outside the airport. First, answer your teacher's questions at Immigration. Then ask your teacher about your suitcase and a taxi.

   2   You arrive in San Francisco International Airport for a three-day conference. You need to make a phone call and you do not have any small change for the public phone. First, answer your teacher's questions at Immigration and then ask your teacher about a public phone and the coins you need to use it.

Language box

We use indirect questions when we want to be more polite:

Where is the bus station?
Can you tell me where the bus station is?

We can use the following at the start of indirect questions:

Do you know ...?
Can you tell me ...?
Could you tell me ...?
Do you have any idea ...?

Indirect questions have a different word order from direct questions:

Where can I make a phone call?
Do you know where I can make a phone call?

travel

Hint

We use the expression **oh dear** to reply to bad news.

I've lost my passport. – Oh dear. When did you last have it?

My suitcase is broken. – Oh dear. How did that happen?

3 Listen again. Tick (✓) the phrases you hear.

a I bought two bottles of spirits in the Duty Free. _____

b What does it look like? _____

c Passengers from outside the EU need to complete a landing card. _____

d Do you know where I can change some money? _____

e Can I have your passport, please? _____

f Can you tell me which flight you were on, please? _____

g Have you any idea how much it costs? _____

h Nobody gave me anything to carry on the plane. _____

4 Match the phrases in **3** with the places below.

Immigration	Baggage reclaim
1	1
2	2
Customs	**Arrivals hall**
1	1
2	2

Writing

1 What problems have you had when flying?

2 Continue this email to a colleague you visited abroad. Tell them what happened when you landed. You can use ideas from **Expressions** or from the list below.

- All the restaurants were closed.
- You took the wrong bus.
- The weather was very bad.
- You left something on the plane.
- Your bags were searched at Customs.

Dear Amy,
Thanks for taking me to the airport yesterday. The flight home was fine, but I had a few problems when I landed.

Best wishes
Jo

What time does the next train leave?

Can you tell me what time the next train leaves?

When there is no question word, we use *if*:

Do you know if I can change money here?

Can you tell me if this bus goes to the centre?

Look

Look again at listening script 34.1 on page 122. Find more examples of indirect questions.

Lesson record

3 new words from this lesson	3 useful phrases from this lesson
1	1 ....
2	2 ....
3	3 ....

Things to remember

....

....

....

....

....

....

How to survive in a hotel

35

In this lesson you will learn language for describing difficulties you may have in a hotel.

Starter

1 In the pictures there are some things you find in a hotel room. Sometimes they can go wrong. Do you know what they are called? If not, how can you describe them?

Expressions

 35.1

1 Listen to three short dialogues. A hotel guest, Irena Alekseeva, has some problems, and talks to reception. She describes three of the items from **Starter**. For each one, write the problem in the table below.

2 Now listen again and write how the receptionist will help in the table below.

Problem	Help from the receptionist
1	
2	
3	

Speaking

1 You are staying in a hotel. You cannot turn the heating down, and your room is too hot. Phone reception (your teacher) and explain the problem.

2 You brought a travel iron with you, and just started ironing your shirt. Suddenly there was a small spark from the iron, and all the lights went out. Find the phone, and explain the situation to reception.

3 You have arrived back at your room with some friends who have a bottle of wine. Unfortunately there is not anything to open it with. Phone the receptionist to ask for help.

Language box

If you want to arrange something, but you do not do it yourself, you can use
to have something done
(*have* + noun + past participle).

> I **had** the car **washed** last week.
> (= someone else / a machine washed it)

> She **has** her hair **done** every Friday.
> (= someone else washes and cuts it)

> They **had** the posters **designed**.
> (= someone else designed them)

You can also use *to get something done* in the same situation, but it is less formal, used more in spoken English or emails:

> I had the room cleaned.
> (= I got the room cleaned)

Hint

If you do not know the name of something, you can describe its use with **It's for ...** or **You use it to ...**
It's for opening wine bottles. (a corkscrew)
You use it to plug electrical things into. (a socket)

3 Listen once more. Complete the sentences with the words used by Irena Alekseeva.

1 Well, _____ the balcony door. I opened it, and now I can't shut it. _____ lock.

2 Could you _____?

3 I'd like, you know, something _____ clothes.

4 Oh, right. _____ now?

5 I can't turn the, um, the _____?

6 You _____ the tap?

Writing

1 You are Irena Alekseeva. You find a feedback form in your hotel room. Fill it in, making comments on some of the things which went wrong.

Hotel feedback form

Your opinion is valuable to us. Please complete the feedback form below marking each category 1–4 (1 = very satisfied, 4 = very unsatisfied).

	1	2	3	4
Prices	☐	☐	☐	☐
Location	☐	☐	☐	☐
Restaurant	☐	☐	☐	☐
Customer service / Staff	☐	☐	☐	☐
Your room (clean, comfortable)	☐	☐	☐	☐
Facilities (TV, films, mini-bar, etc.)	☐	☐	☐	☐

Other comments

_____
_____
_____
_____

You can use *to get someone to do something.* Again, this is also usually used more in spoken English and emails.

> They **got** Marta **to photocopy** the documents.

Look

Look again at listening script 35.1 on page 122. Find more examples of *have / get something done.*

Lesson record

3 new words from this lesson	3 useful phrases from this lesson
1	**1** ....
2	**2** ....
3	**3** ....

Things to remember

....
....
....
....
....

How to eat out

In this lesson you will learn language for talking about and describing food in a restaurant.

Starter

1 Look at these typical dishes from Morocco in the pictures below. Have you ever eaten or tried these dishes? What do you think the ingredients are? Use the words below to help you.

beef   lamb   chicken   fish
curry   rice   pasta   semolina
pastry   cooked vegetables

Expressions

36.1 ○ 1 Listen to three conversations in a restaurant in Morocco. Draw a line to mark the dishes that the customers order.

He She	orders	lamb beef chicken	tajine. kadide. couscous.
They	order	tea water	with mint. with ice.

2 Now listen again. Complete the sentences with the words used to describe food.

1 Semolina? It's _____ wheat.

2 It's _____ slowly cooked mixture of vegetables and meat.

3 Tajine is another _____ casserole.

4 Is it _____ semolina?

5 I can't _____ . It all sounds nice.

6 What do you _____ ?

7 I think _____ that.

8 And what _____ drink: mint tea?

Speaking

1 You are having lunch with your teacher in your country. Your teacher will ask about typical dishes. Decribe them and decide what to order.

2 Now role-play a situation in a restaurant in Morocco with the dishes shown in **Starter**.

Hint

Dish, **course**, and **plate** are words that are easily confused:
dish – a kind of food that is prepared, e.g. lasagne, sushi
course – any of the separate dishes you have in a meal
plate – the thing that you serve the food on

3 Put this dialogue in an Italian restaurant in the correct order.

a _____ I see, and what about this, this orecchiette tricolori? Is that a kind of pasta too?

b _____ It's a kind of pasta, like macaroni but bigger.

c _____ Hmm. It sounds good, but I think I'll have the rigatoni, please.

d _____ And tricolori means 'three colours', I suppose?

e _____ Are you ready to order?

f _____ Yes, the three colours are made with vegetables and herbs.

g _____ Yes, please. What is this, er, rigatoni?

h _____ Yes, it's also a sort of pasta, in the shape of an ear, a little ear.

36.2 **4** Now listen to check your answers.

Writing

1 For your company's in-house magazine, write a short description of how people eat in your county. Describe:

• how many courses people eat
• what traditions there are
• what is acceptable / not acceptable
• what the typical dishes are
• any special rules when eating
• any influences of foreign cuisine in your country's food.

Look

Look again at listening scripts 36.1 and 36.2 on page 122. Find more examples of *will* and *shall*.

Language box

To express a decision that you have just made, we usually use *will*, in contracted form:

I'll have the soup.

We'll have red wine with that, please.

I'll phone you back later, if now isn't a good time.

We'll decide later, if you like.

I'll take the white one, please.

When you are making a suggestion or an offer, you can use *shall*:

Shall we get the bill?

Shall I pay?

Lesson record

3 new words from this lesson

3 useful phrases from this lesson

1 ....   1 ....

2 ....   2 ....

3 ....   3 ....

Things to remember

....
....
....
....
....
....

How to give directions

37

In this lesson you will learn language for giving directions in cities and office buildings.

Starter

1 Write these numbers in words.

1st *first*   2nd   3rd   4th   5th   6th
7th   8th   9th   10th   11th   12th   13th
14th   21st   33rd

2 Match the directions and landmarks with the pictures below.

- turn left
- roundabout
- bridge
- turn right
- traffic lights
- go straight on

Expressions

37.1 1 Listen to Susana talking to Walter, a visitor from Liechtenstein. What is Walter's problem?

37.2 2 Now listen to the rest of Susana and Walter's conversation. Make notes of the directions that Susana gives. Listen again if necessary.

3 Match the questions (1–6) with the answers (a–f).

1 Are you nearly here?
2 Where are you now?
3 How do I get to your office?
4 Where do I go when I come out of the station?
5 Is it far?
6 What do I do when I go into the shopping centre?

a No, it takes about ten minutes.
b You can either take the train or the bus.
c You need to turn left and go up Castellana Street.
d I'm somewhere near Colón.
e First you need to go up the escalator.
f No, I'm afraid I'm a bit lost.

4 Tell your teacher about a situation where you got lost.

travel

Writing

1 Write a reply to the following email.

Subject: Re: Office visit

Dear Bjorn
I'm arriving at the main railway station at 8.15 tomorrow and our meeting doesn't start until 9.30. I'm thinking about walking to your office so I can see some of the city on my trip. How far is it from the station to your office? Which is the best way to go? Can you email me today, so that I have some idea of how long it's going to take? Thanks for your help.
Best wishes

Janine

Hint

Near indicates something is not far away.
My office is near the central bus station.
Nearly means almost or not completely.
We're nearly there. It's just around the corner.

Speaking

1 Where are these places in the city where you work?
- the central bus station
- the main railway station
- the nearest airport
- the best place to take a taxi
- the nearest underground station

2 Role-play this conversation. Your teacher is a visitor from another company and your meeting together has just finished. Your teacher will ask you how to get to the places in 1, and you need to give exact directions. Use as many phrases from **Expressions** and the **Language box** as possible.

Look

Look at listening scripts 37.1 and 37.2 on page 123. Find more examples of verb + preposition to give directions, and *get* meaning *to arrive*.

Language box

When we are giving directions, we often use the verb *go* with *into*, *out of*, *up*, *down*, *over*, *under*, *round*, *across*, and *through*:

Go up in the lift.
Go past the museum.
Go round the corner.

We can also use these prepositions with verbs like *come*, *walk*, *drive*, and *run*:

Come out of the car park.
Walk over the bridge.
Drive down the road.
Run through the park.

We use *get* to talk about arriving somewhere:

Turn right when you get to the top.
Call me when you get here.

Lesson record

3 new words from this lesson	3 useful phrases from this lesson
1	1 ....
2	2 ....
3	3 ....

Things to remember

....
....
....
....
....
....

Travel overview

38

In this lesson you will revise and practise the travel expressions from lessons 34 to 37.

Starter

1 Which of these do you like / dislike? Why?
- arriving in a new place, and not knowing your way around
- staying in a hotel you do not know
- eating out with people you do not know
- going to conferences
- visiting museums and galleries / sightseeing

Instructions

1 You are going to play a travel game. You are at a conference in Newcastle. You will need a counter each and a coin. Toss a coin to move (heads = move one square, tails = move two squares). Each square presents a situation to role-play. You may need to look at the pictures and information to do this. Forfeit squares – go back one square. Lucky squares – go forward one square.

The Sage Gateshead
On Gateshead Quays, the newest place for the best music in the North.

Friday, 7.30pm, Northern Sinfonia
Saturday 7pm – Folk Stars
Saturday 10pm – Late night jazz

Nearest Metro stop: Gateshead, or bus Q1 from Central Station

NIA Newcastle International Airport

Connections
Getting to town

By metro
The metro station is next to the main terminal building. The metro runs every 7 minutes, and the journey takes 23 minutes to Newcastle Central Station.

By bus
To Eldon Square shopping centre (Monument metro stop), central Newcastle, take bus no.75, 76, or 77. Buses run every 30 minutes.

Travel connections

the cellar inn

Starters
Cock-a-leekie soup
Melon with maraschino cherries
Kipper pâté with melba toast

Main
Steak and kidney pie
Mushroom risotto (v)
Northumberland sausage with mashed potato and Yorkshire pudding
Trout with almonds

Desserts
Trifle
Bakewell tart
Apple pie with ice cream or custard

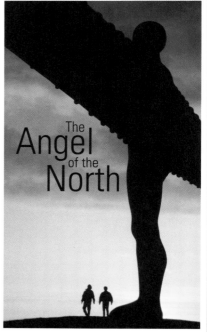

The **Angel** of the **North**

Visit one of Europe's most impressive sculptures, 20m tall, 54m wide.

Directions: Take bus 21, 21A, or 21B from Gateshead bus station.

Journey time: 25 minutes

Angel of the North

Whitefriars Hotel
Grey Street
Newcastle
NE1

travel

START →

FINISH

1 — Your suitcase hasn't arrived. Go to the baggage reclaim, and give your flight and hotel details. See Whitefriars Hotel Information.

2 — You want to get to the town centre. Ask about the metro and buses at the Information Desk. See Map.

3 — Your colleague did not arrive to meet you. Ask where there is a public phone, and what coins you need. See leaflet, Newcastle Airport.

LUCKY — Friends are meeting you at the airport. They offer you a lift into town.

4 — You take a taxi to town. Ask the driver (your teacher) what there is to do and see in Newcastle. See leaflets.

5 — You get to your room, but it's facing the street, so it'll be very noisy. Ask reception for a different room.

17 — Congratulations! You have won the game!

6 — You have a card key to open your door, but you can't find it. Maybe you dropped it. Phone reception to explain the problem.

16 — You want to hear some live music. Ask your partner what's on this weekend. Decide what you want to go to. See leaflet, The Sage.

7 — Your flight is two hours late.

15 — Museums and Galleries are free on Sundays.

FORFEIT

LUCKY — Someone at the conference asks you about your home town. Describe it.

8 — You have some bottles of beer, but nothing to open them with. Phone reception, describing what you want.

14 — You want to see the Angel of the North statue. Ask your partner how to get there! See leaflet, The Angel of the North.

9 — Tomorrow you have to get up very early. You want the hotel to wake you. Phone reception.

10 — You are in a restaurant. Think of three questions you can ask your partner.

13 — Choose a place on the map (in secret). Tell your partner how to get there from the Sage Centre. See map.

12 — The menu doesn't include tax. 17% has been added to the bill!

FORFEIT — You are chatting over dinner. Tell your partner how to cook a famous dish from your country.

11 — Tell your partner about a memorable meal you had once in another country. Describe each course.

10 — Look at the Cellar Inn menu. Give the waiter your order. See leaflet, Cellar Inn Menu.

LUCKY — The restaurant has your favourite English beer.

Map: NEWCASTLE UPON TYNE / GATESHEAD

- University of Newcastle upon Tyne
- Civic Centre
- St James Park (Newcastle United FC)
- Library
- Art Gallery
- PERCY ST.
- NORTHUMBERLAND ST.
- STRAWBERRY PL.
- GALLOWGATE
- m Monument metro
- Eldon Shopping Centre
- MARKET ST.
- Whitefriars Hotel
- CHINATOWN
- CLAYTON ST.
- GRANGER STREET
- GREY ST.
- WESGATE ROAD
- COLLINGWOOD
- St. Marys Cathedral
- NEVILLE ST.
- Castle Keep
- Central Station m
- FORTH ST.
- SWING BRIDGE
- TYNE BRIDGE
- QUAYSIDE
- GATESHEAD QUAYS
- Gateshead Millenium Bridge
- The Sage Gateshead
- Coach Station
- HIGH LEVEL BRIDGE
- River Tyne
- REDHEUGH BRIDGE
- ASKEW ROAD
- Gateshead Metro m
- WEST STREET
- Bus Station
- GATESHEAD

How to **use the present**

In this lesson you will learn how to talk about the present.

Starter

1 Look at the cartoon. Do you like doing these activities in your spare time?

Grammar

39.1 **1** Angela and Robert work for the same company. It is Friday. Listen to their conversation and answer these questions.

    1 What is Robert doing on Saturday?

    2 What does Robert's brother do?

2 What is the connection between Robert's brother, Peter, and these places?

London   ....

Ireland   ....

Kiev   ....

Odessa   ....

Korea   ....

Brazil   ....

3 Complete the sentences with the verbs in **bold**. Then listen again to check your answers.

    1 Is that your brother who **work** in Ireland?

    2 He **work** on a new factory there at the moment.

    3 How long he **be** there?

    4 He always **travel** between the two cities and it's a long way.

    5 He finds that very frustrating. But he **love** Kiev.

Language box

The present simple

We use the present simple to talk about situations that are true, facts, scientific information, and timetables.

> **They export** most of their production to Europe. (= fact)
>
> **Water freezes** at zero degrees centigrade. (= scientific information)
>
> **The first train leaves** at 07.30 a.m. (= timetable)

We also use the present simple for routines or actions that we do regularly.

> **She works** Monday to Friday, but **she never works** at the weekend.

The present continuous

We use the present continuous to talk about actions or situations happening at this moment in time.

> Oh no! Look! **It's raining** again!

We use the present continuous for actions or situations happening around now.

> **The marketing department is preparing** a new brochure.
>
> **The new machine is selling** very well.

We use the present continuous for temporary or provisional situations.

> **We're importing** a lot from Chile because of the situation in Europe.
>
> **They are using** the fax machine because **their server is not working**

grammar

Hint

Use the adverb **always** with the present continuous to show that something makes you angry.
He's always arriving late for meetings.
You're always phoning me about little problems.

6 Anyway he has two more months there and then he **move** to a new project in Korea.

7 What he **do** in his spare time when he's in all these different countries?

8 In the Ukraine he **go out** a lot in the evenings because the people **like** to invite you to their homes.

9 How often you **see** him?

4 Tell your teacher everything you know about Robert's brother.

Remember that stative verbs (*think, know, like, love, hate*, etc.) do not usually use the continuous tense.

I **love** this soup. It tastes delicious.

The present perfect

We can use the present perfect to speak about actions or situations that began in the past and continue now.

I **have worked** for this company for five years. (= I started five years ago and I continue to work for them)

I **haven't seen** him since May.

Practice

1 Complete the sentences with the correct form of the verb.

1 Our company *exports / is exporting* 35% of its production every year.

2 I can't give you a price. I *wait / am waiting* for the new price lists.

3 What *do you do / are you doing* tonight? How about dinner with me?

4 How long *are you working / have you worked* here? About ten years now.

5 *Do you live / Are you living* near your office?

6 How often *does she visit / is she visiting* you? About twice a year.

7 I *don't see / haven't seen* Mary for nearly a year.

8 German people *work / are working* about forty hours per week.

9 How long *is she studying / has she studied* English? Since February last year.

10 Hello? Tom? Listen! I *am waiting / wait* in the car park for you. Hurry up!

Look

Look again at listening script 39.1 on page 123. Find more examples of the present simple, present continuous, and present perfect.

Lesson record

3 new words from this lesson	3 useful phrases from this lesson
1	1 ....
2	2 ....
3	3 ....

Things to remember

....
....
....
....
....
....

How to **use the past**

40

In this lesson you will learn how to talk about the past.

Starter

left   drank   stopped   **ate**

fell   took   met   **went**   looked

put   **got**   parked

rang   **built**   **said**   broke   flew

invited

paid   called   **lost**

arrived

had   **came**   **offered**

told   started

caught   wanted   **won**

gave

drove   **thought**

1   (Circle) the regular past simple forms.
2   Tell your teacher the infinitive of the irregular past simple forms.

Grammar

RALF ZIMMERMANN

ITALIAN FOOD

CV

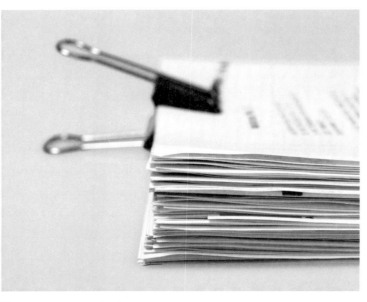

Language box

We use the past simple to describe actions completed at a definite past time. Regular verbs form the past by adding *-(e)d* to the infinitive.

    clean – cleaned   arrive – arrived

    Note: stop – sto*pp*ed   study – stud*i*ed

Irregular verbs have different past forms.

    write – wrote   buy – bought   teach – taught

The past simple of *be* is *was* or *were*.

    It **was** a beautiful day.

    We **weren't** late today.

We form the negative with *did not* and the infinitive:

    I **didn't walk** to work today.

    He **didn't go** to the meeting yesterday.

Hint

The **-ed** ending of regular past simple forms can be pronounced in three different ways.
/t/ finished
/d/ closed
/id/ decided

1 Look at the picture story. What do you think happened?

40.1 2 Listen to Ralf telling the story and underline the verbs you hear in **Starter**.

3 Correct the information in the sentences.

1 He wanted to have lunch in a Chinese restaurant.
2 Ralf left his car on the road.
3 It was raining.
4 Ralf walked to the restaurant.
5 The man was waiting at the restaurant.
6 Ralf invited the man for a drink.
7 The man gave Ralf his mobile number.
8 He said he was looking for a new car.

4 Imagine you are the woman Ralf told his story to. Using the verbs from **Starter** and the phrases you corrected in **3**, tell Ralf's story to your teacher in as much detail as possible.

Practice

1 Make questions to ask Ralf about his story. Put the verb in the past simple or past continuous.

1 Where / have a meeting?
2 What / do with your briefcase?
3 Why / the man call you?
4 What / the man see?
5 What you / offer the man?
6 What / the man look for?

2 Your teacher will ask you the questions. Answer the questions as if you are Ralf.

3 Tell your teacher about a situation where you lost something. Use the questions to help you.

1 Where were you?
2 Who were you with?
3 What did you lose?
4 What were you doing when you lost it?
5 What did you do next?
6 Did you find it in the end?

Look

Look again at listening script on 40.1 page 123. Find more examples of the past simple and past continuous.

We use the auxiliary *did* with the infinitive to form *yes / no* questions:

Did you have a good weekend?
Did you finish the report yesterday?

We use the past continuous for long, unfinished actions in the past. We use *was / were* with *-ing*:

I **was driving** to work at seven o'clock yesterday morning.

They **weren't listening** to the presentation at all.

We often use the past continuous when a past action is interrupted.

We **were having** coffee when the boss walked in.

Lesson record

3 new words from this lesson	3 useful phrases from this lesson
1	1 ....
2	2 ....
3	3 ....

Things to remember

....
....
....
....
....
....

How to **use the future**

In this lesson you will learn how to talk about the future.

Starter

1 What training opportunities does your company offer its staff?
   - language training (which languages?)
   - IT skills
   - management skills
   - communication skills
   - other

Grammar

1 Catherine Fox works as a freelance trainer. She receives the following email. What important information does she get?
   - training topic
   - who is coming to the course
   - training times
   - extra information

 2 Catherine finds three things she is not happy with. She phones the Warsaw office. Write down the changes she wants.

41.1

41.2 **3** Catherine phones back later the same day with some other requests for the training session. Listen, and correct the information in the sentences.

   1 Catherine is taking her laptop to Warsaw.
   2 Catherine is sending the photocopies this week.
   3 They will confirm these requests in writing.
   4 Catherine is taking eggs and string with her to Warsaw.

4 Which tenses are used for the verbs in sentences 1–4 in **3**? Why?

Language box

Will

Use *will* for the future for announcing decisions, and making promises:

> Oh! We haven't got any more coffee. **I'll get some** when I go out.

> He says **he'll finish it** by Friday.

Also use *will* for facts, or when we are certain about something:

> Sandra **will** be thirty next week.

> The elections **will** take place in April.

We use *will* when we expect / believe something to happen, but we are not sure:

> I think **he'll get** the job. He seems the right person for it.

grammar

Hint

We usually use the present continuous with a time phrase, e.g. **on Saturday / at 2.30 / for lunch**.

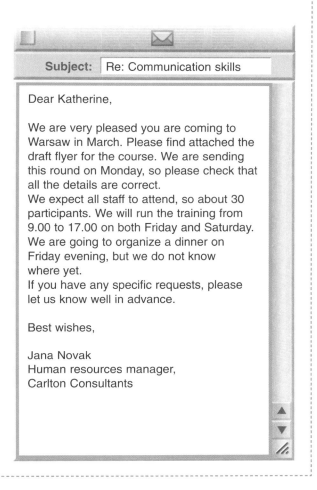

Subject: Re: Communication skills

Dear Katherine,

We are very pleased you are coming to Warsaw in March. Please find attached the draft flyer for the course. We are sending this round on Monday, so please check that all the details are correct.
We expect all staff to attend, so about 30 participants. We will run the training from 9.00 to 17.00 on both Friday and Saturday. We are going to organize a dinner on Friday evening, but we do not know where yet.
If you have any specific requests, please let us know well in advance.

Best wishes,

Jana Novak
Human resources manager,
Carlton Consultants

Practice

1 Write Catherine's email to confirm her requests.

2 Complete the sentences with the correct form of the verb.

1 *We're going to go / We'll go* to Paparazzi's on Friday. Takeshi has booked a table for 8.00 p.m.

2 Hey, look at the forecast for tomorrow. Perfect for the barbecue! *It's being / It's going to be* dry and sunny.

3 What about your summer holiday?
Well, *we're discussing / we discuss* it next week when Alain's back from Paris.

4 Do you have the final schedule?
Oh! I nearly forgot. *I'll get / I'm getting* it right now.

5 Have you had your interview yet?
No. *I'm doing / I'll do* it at 3.00 this afternoon.

6 Right. Monday at 11.00?
Oh, I'm sorry. *I'm doing / I will do* a talk at the University. Is the afternoon any good?

7 I think Adams *is winning / will win* the next election. He's very popular.

Look

Look again at listening scripts 41.1 and 41.2 on pages 123–124, and the email in **Grammar**. Find more examples of *will*, *going to*, and the present continuous used to talk about the future.

Present continuous

We use the present continuous for the future when plans are fixed, or in the diary.

They're spending a weekend in Rome in June.

Are we meeting at 10.30 or 11.30 to discuss the contract?

Going to

Use *going to* to talk about intentions:

I'm going to phone Jack this afternoon to ask where those proofs are.

I'm interviewing this afternoon, so **I'm not going to** answer those emails until tomorrow.

Lesson record

3 new words from this lesson	3 useful phrases from this lesson
1	1 ....
2	2 ....
3	3 ....

Things to remember

....
....
....
....
....
....

How to **make questions**

42

In this lesson you will learn how to form different types of questions.

Starter

How long

How much   **Which**   Whose

How many   **Why**

What   Who   **Where**

When   How   **How far**

1 Find a question word that means:

For what reason?	What price?
What time?	What distance?
What amount of time?	What person?
What number?	What place?

Grammar

1 Sue Bean manages a singer, Carlton. She is arranging some work with the manager of a holiday resort in California. Before you listen, match the questions (1–10) with the answers (a–j).

1   Where's he from?
2   How old is he?
3   What does he look like?
4   Does he play electric or acoustic?
5   Is he reliable?
6   Has he played in resorts before?
7   Who writes his songs?
8   Has he recorded anything?
9   Have you brought a demo CD?
10   Can he play next month?

a   Both.
b   Of course. Here, take a listen.
c   Denver, Colorado.
d   Absolutely. 100%.
e   Probably, it depends on the week.
f   Forty-eight.
g   Not much, he's done hotels and bars mainly.
h   Yes, but not commercially.
i   He does himself, but he does covers too.
j   Well, look, here are some photos.

Language box

Yes / No questions

Questions that have a *yes / no* answer begin with an auxiliary verb. The auxiliary verb comes before the subject.

Are your products fully guaranteed?

Have you met my partner, Silvia López?

Would you like to meet later?

In the present, use *do* when there is no other auxiliary verb.

Do you like your job?

Does Mr Vickery know you're here?

In the past, use *did* when there is no other auxiliary verb.

Did you speak to the manager about this?

Wh- questions

We use an auxiliary verb with question words. The question word and auxiliary verb come before the main verb.

Who does she work for?

When will he leave?

But we do not use the auxiliary *do* when the question word is the subject of the sentence. The *wh-* question word is before the verb.

Who wrote this?
(subject = who, verb = wrote)

What happened?
(subject = what, verb = happened)

Which costs less – the MK5 or the MK17?

grammar

Hint

How come is a very common, easy informal question form. It means **why**.
How come you're working on this?
How come nobody has answered them?

Hint

When the speaker thinks they have understood, but wants to check or express surprise, they can say a sentence and raise their intonation at the end.
You phoned the Head Office?⤴
That's the best you can do?⤴

42.1 ○ **2** Listen to check your answers.

3 Put the questions from the dialogues in the correct order.

1 **Ricky** I like the sound. I like the voice. Let's talk details.

Sue Good. when / want / him / you / play / do / to?

Ricky The third week of next month, from the 15th through the 21st.

2 **Sue** that / the / 21st / to / was / 16th / the?

3 **Ricky** No, from the 15th. he / he / free / isn't / is?

Sue Yeah, he is.

4 **Ricky** play / a / could / twice / he / night?

5 **Sue** Yes, sure. forty-five / each / is / for / minutes / OK / set of songs?

Ricky Fine, forty-five minutes is long enough.

6 **Sue** he / be / playing / in / the / restaurant / would?

Ricky Yes, the first set in the restaurant and the second in the bar.

42.2 ○ **4** Now listen to the second part of the dialogue to check your answers.

Practice

1 Complete the questions with the correct *wh-* question word or the auxiliary verb.

Example __Are__ we meeting tomorrow morning?

1 What _____ your company do?

2 _____ you like to get some coffee?

3 Where _____ we do the interviews?

4 Who _____ this message for me?

5 _____ you ever eaten Korean food?

6 John told me to go home early. _____ he?

7 Where _____ you put my notes?

8 _____ you help me with this, please?

Short questions

We use short questions to show that we are listening and interested.

Tara says we should go.	Does she?
It was a great success.	Was it?

To ask for more information, use a short phrase with a question word.

Can you speak to the client?	Why me?
Mr Dykes wants to see you.	What for?
Betty's leaving the company.	How come?

Look

Look again at listening scripts 42.1 and 42.2 on page 124. Find more examples of the different question forms.

How to **use comparatives**

43

In this lesson you will learn how to use comparatives and superlatives.

Starter

1 Find the pairs of opposite adjectives below.

hard   clean   dangerous   late
rough   light   cheap   cool
long   smooth   slow   quiet
early   interesting dirty   (polite)
bad   new   good   old
soft   expensive   safe   short
noisy   (rude)   boring   quick
heavy   warm

Grammar

43.1 1 Luca and Beatrice are students at an international business school in Zurich, Switzerland. They are talking about possible summer courses. Listen to their conversation and answer the questions below.

1 Which course is Luca going to take?
2 Why is he taking that course?
3 Which is the most expensive course?
4 Is Beatrice going to do the same course?

2 Listen again. Complete the notice with the missing information.

Summer Programme

	Course	Duration	Group	Credits	Price	am	pm
1	Marketing in China	25 hours	24	5	€180	✓	
2	Advertising	24 hours		5			✓
3	International Logistics		50			✓	

All courses begin Monday, July 3rd.

Language box

Short adjectives (*big, cold, slow,* etc.)

These adjectives have one syllable. To make comparatives add *-er* (and *than*).

November is **cold**.
December's usually **colder** (than November).

To make superlatives add *-est*.

But the **coldest** month is January.

There are two important exceptions – *good* (*better, the best*) and *bad* (*worse, the worst*).

Short adjectives (*early, pretty,* etc.)

These adjectives have two syllables. To make comparatives change the *-y* to *-i* and add *-er*.

She's **prettier** than her sister.
I hoped we would finish **earlier**.

To make superlatives add *-iest*.

It was the **easiest** interview I've ever had.

Be careful with the correct spelling. Double the final letter in short adjectives that end in a single consonant (except *slow, new*).

Mexico City is bi**gg**er than Paris.
Bangkok is ho**tt**er than London.

Long adjectives (*important, expensive,* etc.)

These adjectives have two or more syllables. To make comparatives use *more ... than* or *less ... than*.

Diane's a popular manager. She's **more popular** than Tony.

To make superlatives use *the most* or *the least*.

She's probably **the most popular** manager in the company.

The least expensive way to travel is to walk.

grammar

Hint

Use specific information to make an exact comparison.
Petrol is 4% more expensive now than it was in January.
She's three years older than I am.
The price is $12 cheaper now.

3 Match 1–7 with a–g to make complete sentences.

1 The logistics course is
2 The credits in Logistics are
3 That's €60
4 The Logistics group is
5 The group in Advertising is
6 Advertising is the
7 The cost of the Advertising course is €60

a bigger than the other two.
b more valuable than the credits in Marketing.
c longer than Marketing or Advertising.
d more expensive than the Advertising course.
e shortest course.
f smaller than the one in Logistics.
g cheaper than the Marketing course.

4 Describe the three different courses to your teacher. Try to use all the constructions from the **Language box**. Which course is the most interesting for you? Why?

Practice

1 Some of the following sentences are not correct. Put a tick or cross (✓ / ✗) to mark if the sentence is right or wrong. Then correct the mistakes.

1 I think Chinese is more difficult that English. ....
2 I think it's the worst restaurant in town. ....
3 My new car is much more economical than my old one. ....
4 The new price was 5% more low than before. ....
5 I think it's the most sensible thing to do. ....
6 In my opinion, Paris is much more clean than it was ten years ago. ....
7 The weather was more bad last week. ....
8 It's the third biggest textile company in the world. ....
9 If you want, we can take a more early flight. ....
10 He's older as he looks. ....

Look

Look again at listening script 43.1 on page 124. Find more examples of the comparative and *as ... as*.

When things are the same or different:

Use *as ... as* to say that two things are the same (the adjective does not change):

He is **as old as** my brother.
(= they are the same age)

Use *not as ... as* to say that two things are different (the adjective does not change).

The film is **not as good as** the book.
(= in my opinion the book is better than the film)

How to **use the passive**

In this lesson you will learn how to form the passive.

Starter

1   Sarah Radcliffe has to go on a business trip at short notice. Read the email from her colleague and complete it with the words below.

Dear Sarah

Just to let you know that your travel ¹_____ *have all been made*. Your ²_____ application *is being processed* and we should receive it soon. The ³_____ *has been booked* – your itinerary *is attached*. You *will be picked up* by ⁴_____ at 6am. The ⁵_____ *has been organized* too – it's at the Ambassador in Mumbai. Jhoti will meet you at the airport and take you there.

Regards
Meta

- visa
- taxi
- flight
- hotel
- arrangements

2   What do the verb forms in *italics* have in common?

Grammar

1   Read the active sentences below. Tell your teacher which tense each sentence is.

1   Printers printed this book in Portugal.
2   We are processing your application for a visa.
3   A Dutch scientist first identified the virus.
4   Orange growers grow oranges here.
5   Writers have written a lot of books about this period.
6   Someone built this pyramid around the year 2000 BC.
7   The President of France opened the bridge in 2005.
8   Iberia have cancelled Iberia flight 413 to Bilbao due to bad weather.

Language box

The passive is a verb phrase made with *be* + past participle. *Be* changes its form according the verb tense.

We use the passive when we do not know who is responsible for an action. We also use the passive when it is obvious who is responsible for the action, or when it is not necessary.

The present simple passive:
Olive oil **is made** in most Mediterranean countries.

The present continuous passive:
Two men **are being questioned** by police.

The past simple passive:
She **was asked to** become director of the institute.

The past continuous passive:
The company **was being sold** by the owners, but we didn't know.

The present perfect passive:
Our flight **has been cancelled** because of the bad weather.

The future passive (*will / going to*):
The project **will be financed by** the United Nations.

grammar

Hint

You can also make the passive with **get** (in informal or spoken style) instead of **be**.
Everyone will get invited to the staff dinner, don't worry.
Four people got injured in the factory last month.

44.1 **2** Listen and write sentences 1–8 in **1** in the passive. Then practise saying them.

3 Match definitions (a–d) with sentences (1–8) in **2**. Some definitions work with more than one sentence. We use the passive (not the active):

a when we want to emphasize the action more than the person who does the action

b when we want a neutral, impersonal style

c when we do not know who does the action (who the agent is)

d when it is obvious who does the action.

44.2 **4** Marga, who works in an accounts department, is receiving a call from her company's bank. Listen to the dialogue and correct her notes.

Phone Open Enterprises urgently about a cheque that their bank is still waiting for. It was the one that I deposited on Thursday and it was signed by someone called Simon Weston.

Practice

1 Rewrite these sentences to make the word in *italics* the focus of the sentence. Decide if it is necessary to say who did the action.

Example: The Human Resources manager interviews *candidates*.

Candidates are interviewed by the Human Resources manager.

1 The company provides *free accommodation* for some staff.

2 Someone is translating *the presentation* into Japanese.

3 People across the Arab world drink *camel's milk*.

4 Musicians made *this recording* in Casablanca.

5 They completed *their research* two weeks ago.

6 The police have not closed *the city centre* during the G8 conference.

7 We launched *this product* in 2003.

8 The owners will sell *this land* to developers for €500,000.

9 The IT department are going to fix *my PC* tomorrow.

10 They are not going to offer *Ivan* the job of department manager.

In the passive when we say who did the action, we use *by*.

The stadium **was designed by** a Japanese architect.

Any decision **will be made by** Head Office.

Look

Look again at **Starter**, and listening script 44.2 on page 124. Find more examples of the passive.

Lesson record

3 new words from this lesson	3 useful phrases from this lesson
1	1 ....
2	2 ....
3	3 ....

Things to remember

....

....

....

....

....

....

reading bank

PIN numbers

1 You are going to read some advice about how to remember the secret number or PIN we need for our bank cards. PIN means *Personal Identification Number*. We can also say *PIN number*.

Read the article once and look at the advice below. Put a tick (✓) for good advice and a cross (✗) for bad advice.

1 Use your birthday as a PIN. _____

2 Use the same number for all your cards. _____

3 Change your PIN every year. _____

4 Combine the years of two important moments in history to make a PIN. _____

5 Invent a PIN using two important numbers from your life. _____

6 Think of a sentence with the same number of words as your PIN. _____

7 Use your imagination to help you remember the number. _____

8 Always give your PIN number to the police when they ask for it. _____

2 Read the article again and choose the best answers.

1 The thieves stole the man's
   a bank cards.
   b official documents.
   c wallet containing his bank cards and documents.

2 They discovered his date of birth, because
   a it was on a piece of paper in his wallet.
   b it was on his driving licence.
   c the man gave it to them on the phone.

3 Elvis Presley died
   a in 1977.
   b in 1980.
   c the same year as John Lennon.

4 If you forget your PIN at the cash machine you should
   a imagine yourself writing the number down.
   b look at the keypad and remember the position of the numbers.
   c call the police.

5 If you lose your bank card, the police
   a will always ask you for your PIN.
   b will only ask for your PIN by phone.
   c will never ask for your PIN by phone.

3 Mark the sentences true (T) or false (F).

1 The thieves stole €5,000 from the man's wallet. _____

2 The man's bank has said it will give him the money back. _____

3 The man used a different PIN for each of his cards. _____

4 More men than women use the same PIN for all of their cards. _____

5 Most people change their PIN every year. _____

6 Psychologists can help you remember your PIN. _____

7 You can often remember the position of your PIN on the keypad. _____

8 You should call the police with your PIN if you lose your credit cards. _____

4 Match the words (1–8) with the definitions (a–h).

1 wallet
2 cardholder
3 survey
4 significant
5 pattern
6 digit
7 withdraw
8 account

a important
b take money out of the bank
c a small bag for cards, money, and documents
d place where you have your money in a bank
e questionnaire
f an arrangement of lines, shapes, etc.
g number
h a person who has a bank card

PIN numbers

To make our lives even more difficult, banks are now recommending not using your date of birth as a PIN number. One unfortunate cardholder, who used his birthday as a PIN, had his bank card stolen along with his driving licence and all the other documents contained in his wallet. When the thieves entered his date of birth as a PIN at a cash machine, they managed to withdraw nearly €5,000 from his account. His bank says they will not return his money because he chose the wrong PIN. A further mistake this cardholder made was to use the same PIN for all of his cards. An Internet security survey discovered that people often choose the same PIN for all their cards, although more women than men do this. The same survey also shows that eight out of ten people never change their PIN, although all banks suggest changing it at least once a year.

But how is it possible to remember so many different numbers? A group of leading psychologists has made a list of some useful suggestions for choosing and remembering PINs, some of which are listed below:

- Divide your PIN into two parts and choose two significant events, for example the years of Elvis Presley's and John Lennon's deaths (7780).

- Choose numbers which mean something to you, like your age when you had your first child, or your mother's house number (2831).
- Think of a phrase where each word has the same number of letters as the one you need to remember. For example, you could use: Don't (4) forget (6) your (4) PIN (3) to remember the PIN 4643.
- Close your eyes and imagine yourself writing the number in red ink on white paper.
- Visualize the pattern the digits make on the keypad. Your brain can remember the position of the buttons even if you are not sure of the numbers.

And one last piece of advice: be extremely careful, if you receive a call about your PIN number, if your cards have been stolen. Credit card companies and the police will never ask you for your PIN, so do not give it to anyone on the phone.

Glossary

Internet security protecting secret information online
psychologist a person who studies the mind and how it works
phrase a group of words used together
visualize when you imagine a picture in your mind
keypad numbered buttons that you can press on a cash machine

reading bank

How old did you say?

1 You are going to read about age in the workplace. Read the text quickly and decide what the main idea of the text is. Age is a problem because:

  a both older and younger employees have to deal with prejudice in the workplace.

  b older workers cannot adapt to new situations and are not up to date.

  c younger workers are too inexperienced to be managers.

2 Match a title with each paragraph a–d.

  1 Advice for job seekers

  2 'I hide the past'

  3 Look on the bright side

  4 'But I'm the managing director'

3 Match the words (1–8) with the definitions (a–h).

  1 potential

  2 to matter

  3 up to date

  4 overlook

  5 irrelevant

  6 property development

  7 ageism

  8 kid

  a not important

  b modern

  c a child or young adult

  d not notice, not see

  e to be important

  f the business of building or improving buildings

  g having pre-formed ideas about people because of their age

  h possible

4 Mark the sentences true (T) or false (F).

  1 According to Pippa Jameson, everybody knows age is important when looking for jobs. _____

  2 According to Pippa, employers think older people do not know how to use modern equipment and software. _____

  3 Judith Randall wants a similar job to her present one. _____

  4 Judith tells employers about every company that she has worked for. _____

  5 John Clennell has no age-related problems because he is only twenty-six. _____

  6 John Clennell thinks that clothes are very important in his job. _____

  7 Pippa advises younger employees to include work that they did for free on their CV. _____

  8 Pippa thinks that education needs to be at the top of a young person's CV. _____

How old did you say?

Do you include your age in your CV? Some people do. Some people don't. But it's usually possible for employers to work out how old you are from other information, such as educational details. But what effect does your age have on potential employers? Pippa Jameson, a recruitment consultant for Smythson Placement Services, London, says it matters more than you think. 'Unfortunately employers can often have fixed ideas about people of a certain age group. They sometimes feel that older people are not up to date with current technology, or that younger people can't accept managerial responsibility. The situation is improving, but it's a very slow process.'

a _____

Judith Randall is 54 and has worked in sales for thirty years. She has a lot of management experience, but is unhappy with her current job. She'd like to find a new management position, but she's concerned that potential employers could overlook her experience, because of her age. 'I do feel that older workers get a raw deal in the recruitment process – you really have to sell yourself, because you're competing with people half your age. I am very careful about what I include in my CV. I've taken out irrelevant information – say, everything over twenty years old. So for example I don't mention companies that I've worked for that have gone out of business.'

b _____

John Clennell is 26 and is the managing director of a property development company. Despite his success he still finds ageism in the workplace. 'When I'm on a visit with a client, people will often assume that the client is the manager, because my clients are usually older than me. It's really frustrating! I do everything I can to make people believe I'm older than I am – I always dress quite formally, for example. Most people wouldn't think this was a problem at all, but it is really annoying to be seen as a kid when you want to be taken seriously.'

c _____

So what can you do? Pippa Jameson advises her older clients to do what Judith did and remove their age from their CV, as well as old information. 'Make sure your CV is up to date, relevant, and specific to the job you're applying for. Emphasize your IT skills and take advantage of training to show that you're not afraid to learn new things'. She says that younger job hunters should try to have a more serious image. 'Highlight your experience – even if it was unpaid, voluntary work. Put all the details of your education at the end of your CV, so it's not the first thing employers see. And prepare what you want to say in your interview, so that you seem mature and articulate – don't use slang!'

d _____

Her final advice for both older and younger workers? 'Don't view your age as a problem, but as something positive. If you can see your age and experience, or your youth and enthusiasm, as a bonus, employers will too.'

Glossary

recruitment consultant a person who finds employees for companies
a raw deal when people treat you badly or unfairly
slang casual, informal language. The words people use with their friends

reading bank

New York cabbie

1 You are going to read about Melissa Plaut, a taxi driver in New York, who also has her own blog. A *blog* is a personal website where you can write about your own experiences and opinions. Read the article and answer the questions.

1 Why does the writer say that Melissa Plaut is brave?

_____

2 What does she do when people shout at her?

_____

3 Where does she show her photographs?

_____

4 Who helped Melissa when the teenagers did not pay?

_____

5 Who does Melissa write about on her blog?

_____

6 What two qualities help Melissa in her job?

_____

2 Number the people in the order they are mentioned.

a _____ a man who changed his mind about Melissa's driving

b _____ a driver who did not want to wait his turn at the airport

c _____ a doctor who used to drive a taxi

d _____ a girl who could not hear well

e _____ an aggressive taxi driver who hit her car

f _____ some teenagers who did not want to pay

g _____ a passenger who was smoking in her taxi

h _____ someone who could not speak that day

3 Mark the sentences true (T) or false (F).

1 Melissa never has problems with pedestrians. _____

2 Passengers cannot smoke in Melissa's taxi. _____

3 When someone threatens Melissa she takes a photo of them. _____

4 Melissa never breaks the rules. _____

5 Melissa is a very negative cabbie. _____

6 Melissa likes her job although it is dangerous. _____

4 Find the words in the text that match the following definitions:

1 a person who rides in a taxi _____

2 violent _____

3 to try and frighten someone _____

4 a line of people waiting _____

5 a photograph _____

6 problems _____

7 the place you are going to _____

8 saying sorry _____.

Melissa Plaut: New York cabbie

You have to be brave to be a taxi driver in New York City, and even more so if you're a woman. But nothing seems to frighten Melissa Plaut. In a typical week she has to deal with passengers who refuse to pay her, aggressive drivers who insult and threaten her, and arrogant pedestrians who don't look before they step off the kerb.

However, Melissa has her own way of dealing with difficult situations. When a passenger gets angry because she won't let him

smoke in her taxi, she just throws him out and takes photographs of him shouting at her through the closed window. Later that night she posts the photos on her blog, www.newyorkhack.blogspot.com, so that everyone can see him making a fool of himself. She does the same with an impatient van driver who won't wait in the queue, and tries to get to the airport first. And the cabbie who stops his car, gets out, and bangs on the window of her taxi with his hand. If anyone tries to

frighten Melissa, she's ready with her camera to get a shot of their face and show it to the rest of the world.

But Melissa isn't looking for trouble, and in general she doesn't break the rules – except when a group of teenagers get out of her taxi without paying, Melissa goes after them. With the help of a police officer she makes them pay.

Yet Melissa does not only write about her nightly conflicts on the blog. She tells stories about all the different people she meets, like the deaf girl who asked for paper and a pencil to write down her destination, the woman who left taxi-driving to become a doctor, and the woman who had just been to the dentist and couldn't pronounce her words properly. Reading her experiences makes you realize just how much Melissa actually likes people. She can usually find something positive to say even if the night has gone badly, and if a passenger is angry when they enter her cab, she can often change their mood. One man told her she was a terrible driver at the start of his journey and ended up apologizing and giving her a big tip when he got out of her taxi.

It's clear Melissa enjoys living life in the fast lane. With her sense of humour and spirit of adventure, she's sure to go far.

Glossary

cabbie another word for a taxi driver
kerb the edge of the pavement where it meets the road
tip the extra money you give for good service
lane a separate part of the road for traffic to drive on
pedestrian a person who is walking in the street, rather than driving
to go far to be very successful in your life

reading bank

Larger than life

1 You are going to read some short texts about people who achieved a lot in their chosen field, but died very young. Read the texts quickly and match them to the images.

2 Read text **a** and mark the sentences true (T) or false (F).

1 Charlie Parker started a new jazz movement with Dizzy Gillespie. _____

2 He started playing the trumpet when he was thirteen. _____

3 His private life was not as successful as his professional life. _____

4 He died in 1965. _____

3 Read text **b** and mark the sentences true (T) or false (F).

1 Rudolph Valentino didn't plan from an early age to be in film. _____

2 He lived in three countries. _____

3 His film career was uninterrupted. _____

4 His death came when he was enjoying great professional success. _____

4 Read text **c** and mark the sentences true (T) or false (F).

1 Fabio Casartelli had little success as a cyclist. _____

2 He rode for more than one team. _____

3 He died of head injuries. _____

4 There is a memorial to Fabio in a church.

5 Read text **d** and mark the sentences true (T) or false (F).

1 Eva Perón came from a rich family. _____

2 She met Juan Perón in Buenos Aires. _____

3 She gave up acting when she became First Lady. _____

4 Everyone loved her. _____

6 Answer the questions about all the texts. There may be more than one answer to each question.

1 Who died the youngest?

2 Who left their own country permanently?

3 Who became a parent?

4 Who died of an illness?

5 Who had problems with drugs?

6 Who left home at a very early age?

Charlie Parker a

Born in Kansas in 1920, Charlie Parker, nicknamed "Yardbird" (or "Bird" for short), was one of the creators of bebop jazz in the 1940s. He began playing the alto saxophone in 1933 and played in different bands before meeting Dizzy Gillespie in New York City. They formed a quintet in 1945 and became the leaders of the bebop movement in jazz. Parker's brilliant improvisations, noted for their power and beauty, were soon admired by thousands of musicians. He composed several instrumental quartets, made many recordings, and played with Miles Davis and many other famous jazz musicians. He married and had a daughter, but his personal life was troubled, and he was addicted to drugs and alcohol. Parker's death at the age of 35 from pneumonia, cut short his career and made him a legend. The words "Bird lives" appeared as graffiti in the New York subway just hours after his death.

Glossary

nickname a name your friends or family call you
quintet a group with five musicians
legend somebody who is very admired by later generations

Rudolph Valentino b

Cinema's original 'Latin Lover' was Rudolph Valentino, born in Castellaneta, Italy in 1895. After studies at military academy and agricultural college he moved to Paris at the age of 17 and a year later to New York, where he worked as a gardener, dishwasher, tango dancer, and occasional petty criminal. Through a friend he got a job dancing in a musical. He also played small parts in films, usually a Latino villain. In *The Four Horseman of the Apocalypse* (1921), his good looks and charm were a great hit with the public, and in *The Sheik* (1921) his magnetic personality made him a star. After a series of mediocre films he took a two-year break, writing and publishing poetry. He returned to films shortly afterwards in *The Eagle* (1925) and *The Son of the Sheik* (1926) and later that year was hospitalized with a perforated ulcer. There were complications, and on August 23, 1926, the 31-year-old actor died of peritonitis and septic endocarditis. Mass hysteria surrounded his death, with rumours of some fans committing suicide. An estimated 80,000 people visited Campbell's New York funeral parlour to see his body.

Glossary

petty criminal not famous or involved in big crimes
villain a criminal, an evil person
mediocre average, not very good

Fabio Casartelli c

Fabio Casartelli was born on August 1st 1970 in Italy. He showed great promise as an amateur competitive cyclist, winning a gold medal in the 1992 Olympic road race, when he beat Dutch rider Erik Dekker to first place by one second. In 1993 he turned professional and joined the Aristoea team, riding in the Tour of Switzerland and the Giro d'Italia. He moved to the Motorola team in 1995 and at the age of twenty-four was selected for the Tour de France. On July 18th, Fabio Casartelli and other riders crashed on the descent of the Col de Portet d'Aspet in the Pyrenees. Fabio had heavy facial and head injuries and lost consciousness. While being taken to hospital by helicopter ambulance, Fabio stopped breathing and after numerous resuscitation attempts was declared dead. The Motorola team decided to continue with the Tour and the rest of the competitors paid tribute to Fabio by letting his teammates cross the finish line of the next stage side by side. Riders donated all money won that day to his family – Fabio's wife had recently given birth to their son. The Société du Tour de France erected a memorial to Fabio on the spot where he crashed and the bicycle he was riding at the time was placed in the chapel at Madonna del Ghisallo, site of a Catholic shrine and cycling museum near his home.

Glossary

amateur to take part in a sport without payment
to resuscitate to make someone start breathing again
memorial a statue or stone to remind people of a famous person or event

Eva Perón d

Eva Maria Ibarurgen Duarte was born into a humble home in Los Toldes, Argentina in 1919, the youngest of five children. Her father died when she was seven and the family struggled financially. In 1935, aged fifteen, she went to Buenos Aires to become an actress. In 1944 at a benefit for earthquake victims in San Juan she met Juan Perón. She was a popular stage, screen, and radio actress by this time and he was a leading politician. They got married in 1945. In 1946 he was elected to the presidency. Eva devoted all her time as First Lady to the poor of Argentina and over the next seven years brought the working classes into a position of political power. She got women the vote and legalized divorce. Evita, as she became known, was a controversial figure, loved by the working classes, but feared and hated by some, who believed she was using her public position for personal gain. Her death from cancer at age 33 helped to fix her popularity in the public consciousness and millions lined the streets of Buenos Aires for her funeral. She has become an icon and the subject of many books, films, and a musical.

Glossary

humble having a low position in society
to struggle to find it difficult to do something
icon a famous person who becomes a symbol

reading bank

Edi Rama, mayor of Tirana

1 You are going to read a text about Edi Rama, the mayor of Tirana, Albania. Mark the sentences true (T) or false (F).

1 Twenty years ago, there was almost no communication between Albania and other countries. _____

2 The population of Albania is lower now than it was twenty years ago. _____

3 Edi Rama has always been a politician. _____

4 Edi Rama liked Paris because it was like his own city, Tirana. _____

5 The first thing Edi Rama did when he became mayor was open a cinema. _____

6 The centre of Tirana used to be a large park. _____

7 Edi Rama painted the buildings in bright colours himself. _____

8 Everyone is very pleased with what Edi Rama has done. _____

9 Edi Rama has already started working on projects outside the capital. _____

10 Edi Rama's next major project is to develop the airport. _____

2 Match the words (1–10) with the definitions (a–j).

1 architect
2 apartment block
3 bodyguard
4 boulevard
5 to cheer up
6 high-rise block
7 mosque
8 shortage
9 suburbs
10 supplies

a building where Muslims worship
b not enough of something
c area near the city with many houses, but away from the centre
d a very tall building with many floors
e to make someone feel less sad
f a building with flats on different floors
g things (e.g. food, water) that you need to live, or do an activity
h someone who protects an important person (from being attacked)
i someone who designs buildings
j wide city street

3 Complete the summary with the words below.

basics	buildings	contact
disappointed	Paris	pleased
regions	Tirana	

For many years, Albania had almost no
[1] _____ with other countries, but in the last few years it has opened up to the West. The capital Tirana is now a busy city, with parks and trees and brightly coloured
[2] _____. Edi Rama, once an artist living in [3] _____, is the person responsible. First when he came back, he was Minister of Culture. Later he became mayor of Tirana. Most people are very [4] _____ with the changes, but some still complain about
[5] _____ such as water and electricity. Meanwhile, those in [6] _____ outside the city are [7] _____ that they cannot benefit from the improvements of the capital. Nevertheless, Rama is making changes in other towns in Albania too, but he also has plans to make the centre of [8] _____ look even better.

Glossary

to ban to say officially that people must not do something
concrete hard substance used for building, made by mixing cement, sand, small stones, and water
concrete jungle an unpleasant part of a city where there are a lot of ugly buildings close together
derelict a building or piece of land that is empty, not used, and in a bad condition
façade the front of a large building
isolated far away from other places, with no international communication

Edi Rama, mayor of Tirana

When you hear someone say 'Albania', many people think of a country with no outside communication, and fifty years behind the times. Or maybe they remember the Albanians who left by boat for Italy. Until recently, Albania was isolated from the rest of the world. Modern art and jazz were banned. In fact, anything 'beautiful' was thought of as bad. Until the mid 90s, the capital, Tirana, was just a small concrete jungle of a quarter of a million people, with bicycles and horses, but few cars.

Albania is still one of the poorest countries in Europe, but Tirana's population has grown, and it is now a busy centre of trade and industry. After fifty years of communism and ten years of capitalism, Tirana is beginning to see the light of day. Edi Rama, the son of Albania's most famous sculptor, Kristaq Rama, and now the country's most popular politician, has done more to cheer up the people of Tirana than anyone else. He first showed an interest in politics in the early 1990s as leader of the Albanian young democracy movement.

But that didn't last long. In 1995 Rama went to Paris, where he studied art and sold his paintings. With money from his art shows he travelled around Europe. He was shocked. Why wasn't Tirana such a great city as London or Paris? Rama decided to transform his hometown into something special.

By chance, in 1998, Rama returned to Tirana for his father's funeral, and he was asked to become Minister of Culture. Although he had no ambitions to go back into politics, Rama took the job. The first thing he did was to open a cinema in Tirana, and bring in films from Hollywood, all of which had been banned.

In 2000, Rama was elected mayor of Tirana. He cleaned up the city by taking away thousands of tons of concrete and rubbish. He planted 4,000 trees and put up streetlights. The centre of the city, which used to be home to derelict buildings, is now a large, leafy park where families picnic, and the wide streets are full of cafés where locals drink coffee, just as in any fashionable European city.

But the most striking thing about the city is the colour. You no longer see sad, grey concrete housing blocks. Rama asked local artists to paint the façades of the apartment blocks, which now shine brightly with sky blue, sunflower yellow and Moroccan pink – rather like a Mondrian painting.

In Tirana now there's generally a feeling of optimism, and the changes seem to have helped the country progress. But in other Albanian cities there's a lot of anger. They, too, want a cinema, or a football pitch. Even within his own party, the Socialists, some say that the quality of life hasn't improved. Others complain that Rama hasn't spent enough time looking at basic problems such as drinking water and electricity shortages. In fact, some are so angry, that now Rama has a bodyguard because his life has been threatened twice.

In the last few years, Edi Rama has renovated the airport, and built roads, schools, and playgrounds in the suburbs. Electricity and water supplies have also improved. But these projects need money. Much of the city's work was done free by local construction companies, and Rama has also raised money from the EU, World Bank, UNDP, and Soros Foundation, but it's not enough, and Tirana's state budget is getting smaller and smaller.

Rama's plan now is to rebuild the city centre. For this, he has invited architects from all over Europe to design high-rise blocks for Skanderbeg Square, near Parliament. But still some argue that the new buildings will block their view of the mosque and the clock tower – both of which Rama restored. Others say they will lose sight of Mount Dajte.

But despite the complaints, Rama believes he is right, and loves his work. 'It's the most exciting job in the world, because I get to invent and to fight for good causes every day.' And he can continue his artistic work on a grand scale. Maybe, as some say, the capital will one day be renamed 'TiRama'.
www.time.com/time/europe/hero2005/rama.html

reading bank

Working women of the world

1 You are going to read about five women from different countries. They were asked about their jobs and daily routines. Read the texts quickly and tick (✓) the correct name or names.

Who	Annette	Aysegul	Ewa	Ingrid	Sue
1 says that she enjoys her work?					
2 has problems with her boss or workmates?					
3 uses public transport to get to work?					
4 spends the most time travelling?					
5 spends the least time travelling?					
6 has the longest working day?					
7 sometimes works at the weekend too?					
8 has the most flexibility about work time?					
9 is involved with education in some way?					

Annette Dalsgaard
lecturer in midwifery, Denmark

I work as a lecturer in Midwifery, and I really love my work. Officially I work thirty-seven hours a week, or seven hours and twenty-four minutes a day, which is the standard working week in Denmark. However, in fact I work much more than that, approximately sixty hours a week. When I have most work, the busiest time, is at the end of the semesters in January and June. I live a very long way from work and it takes me six hours a day on public transport by bus and train to get there and to get home. I normally use this time for preparation. On Saturdays I have a chance to spend time with my children, husband, and friends.

Aysegul Kina
product development engineer, USA

On average I work eleven to thirteen hours a day, plus Saturdays and some Sundays. I don't get paid for overtime, because I'm in management. My commute takes a minimum of ninety minutes a day. The traffic is always bad on the highway and I hate being in traffic. I used to walk to my office back in Istanbul and it was so lovely – I could stop and buy nuts, fruit juice, and fruit on my way to work. Here I don't like the working hours, I hate twelve hours with no fresh air. The office feels like a prison. We have our lunch alone, there's no friendship over lunch. We're in the middle of nowhere, so if you want to go out for lunch it takes half an hour to go anywhere. And we have restrictions on the shoes we can wear (no high heels, no open toes), which I hate. But I like my position in the company.

Ewa Krosnicka
judicial assistant, Poland

This kind of work doesn't depend on time. When you work in a court, you have two sessions a week, so a few days earlier you have to read all the cases carefully. Usually we begin at 08.30 and the last case of the day is at 14.30. During the week there are a lot of routine things you have to do: co-ordinating arrests with the police, judgements, working on the legal grounds for a judgement, and writing the judgement, which is normally done after the trial. Working on a judgement is something that I do at home. After work you sit at home until quite late writing up sentences, on Saturdays and Sundays too, even though courts are closed on Saturdays. Travel? Well, where I live it takes me about twenty-five minutes by motorbike or forty by bus.

Glossary
lecturer a teacher at a university (or similar institution)
midwifery helping women to give birth to babies

Glossary
overtime working more hours than you are contracted to work
commute the time you spend travelling to and from work

Glossary
court a place where civil and criminal disputes are resolved
case a civil or criminal dispute
sentence the final decision of the court

Ingrid Marcela Jara
web-page designer, Cuba

I work as a web-page designer in a travel agency. I start work at eight o'clock in the morning and I finish at five, with an hour for lunch, usually from about twelve to one. That's quite typical for people who work behind the scenes in the tourist industry in my country. Luckily, I don't have to come to work at the weekend, but sometimes I have to travel around the country for two weeks at a time. It takes me about an hour to get to work by bus. What I don't like about my job is all the paperwork, and sometimes my boss treats me like a secretary. What I do like is being able to travel and see the island and learning new things about my job.

Glossary
paperwork office work, not physical work
behind the scenes doing work that customers do not see

Sue Gardiner
freelance art lecturer and writer, New Zealand

I'm self-employed, so there are many different aspects to my work, and I like that. I write for art publications. I'm a director of an art collection. I edit the collection website and teach Art at Auckland University, taking people around art galleries every month. I work from home but I travel every week into the city centre to visit galleries, artists' studios, editors, and libraries. I like my work hours because they're flexible, giving me time for family and travel. I have to be self-motivated and always look for new work opportunities. I spend a lot of time alone at the computer, but I also visit galleries and meet students. My weekends are for friends and family, but I occasionally work then. I started writing when my children were small, and I work with my father on the art collection, and that has special challenges and benefits.

Glossary
gallery place where artists show or sell their work
flexible not fixed, can be changed if necessary
self-motivated when a person is interested in their own work

2 Find a word in the text that means:

1 normal, the most typical (Annette) ....
2 part of a university year (Annette) ....
3 making or having friends (Aysegul) ....
4 very nice (Aysegul) ....
5 most common, everyday (Ewa) ....
6 a process to decide if someone is guilty (Ewa)

....
7 to prepare writing or pictures for publication (Sue)

....
8 things that are difficult, that make you work hard (Sue)

....
9 advantages or useful effects (Sue) ....
10 working for yourself (Sue) ....

3 Who is it? Match these descriptions with one of the people in the texts.

1 She is very independent, and can organize her own time. ....
2 Her company does not allow her to wear exactly what she wants. ....
3 She does not like the routine aspects of her job, but is happy. ....
4 Her family are probably happy when the weekend comes. ....
5 Sometimes she uses public transport. Sometimes she uses her own transport. ....
6 She often does not know how much time her next piece of work will need. ....

4 Mark the sentences true (T) or false (F).

1 Annette prepares her classes at home at the weekend.

....
2 Ewa's home is an extension of her office. ....
3 Ingrid is depressed when her employer sends her on a trip. ....
4 Sue works part of the time with both her parents. ....
5 Aysegul buys lunch on her way to work. ....

listening bank

Sudoku: business or pleasure?

You are going to listen to an interview with an expert on sudokus. A *sudoku* is a number puzzle, where you have to write the numbers one to nine in each row, each column, and each grid, without repeating a number. Listen to the recording as many times as you need to and try to answer the questions. The recording is on the MultiROM at the back of this Student's Book.

1 Mark the sentences true (T) or false (F).

1 The sudoku originally came from Japan.

2 The puzzle was popular in Japan in the eighteenth century. _____

3 A New Zealand judge wrote a computer program that makes sudokus. _____

4 He makes a lot of money from his computer program. _____

5 A Japanese company, Nikoli, employs people who write sudokus by hand. _____

6 Nikoli supplies all Japanese newspapers and magazines with sudokus. _____

7 A French castle offers sudoku holidays.

8 Sudokus are very educational, especially for children. _____

2 Listen again. Who are these people?

- Kieran Golding _____
- Leonhard Euler _____
- Maki Kaji _____
- Wayne Gould _____

3 Now listen again and answer the questions.

1 What was the name of Dell magazine's sudoku puzzle?

2 Where did the New Zealand judge find a book of sudokus?

3 How many countries buy sudokus from Wayne Gould?

4 How many people work for Nikoli Publishing?

5 How many countries does Nikoli publish sudoku books in?

6 Where can you do sudokus on the sudoku holiday in France?

7 What makes one sudoku fan depressed?

8 Why should teachers use sudokus in the classroom?

4 Match the words 1–8 with the definitions a–h.

1 puzzle
2 to spread
3 by chance
4 on the spot
5 abroad
6 an addict
7 depressed
8 to concentrate

a in other countries
b a person who cannot stop doing something
c a game using words or numbers
d very sad and without hope
e without planning
f to pay a lot of attention to something
g to move to more places
h immediately

listening bank

Karl Bushby

You are going to listen to a news story about Karl Bushby. Listen to the recording as many times as you need to and try to answer the questions. The recording is on the MultiROM at the back of this Student's Book.

1 Listen to the news story about Karl Bushby and answer the questions.

1 Where is Karl Bushby from?

_____

2 What is he trying to do?

_____

3 How old is he?

_____

4 Where is he now?

_____

5 What is his problem?

_____

2 Complete the summary of Karl's journey with the missing information.

Karl Bushby **The Goliath Expedition**

One man walking alone, around the world, crossing
a _____ countries, one frozen sea,
b _____ deserts, and c _____
mountain ranges. Here are the facts.
date of departure   d _____
date of arrival   e _____
total distance   f _____ miles
starting in   Punta Arenas, g _____
finishing in   Hull, h _____
more information   www.goliath.mail2web.com

3 Complete the sentences with the correct tense of the verb in brackets. Listen to the recording again to check your answers.

Karl Bushby ¹_____ (be) now thirty seven years old. After eleven years in the British Army he ²_____ (decide) that he wanted to do something different, something that no other person ³_____ (do) before. He ⁴_____ (realize) that he could walk non-stop from Punta Arenas in Chile, South America, to his home in Hull in England. With the help of his father and a close friend , Karl ⁵_____ (begin) what he ⁶_____ (call) the Goliath Expedition in November 1998. He ⁷_____ (complete) seventeen thousand miles already. He ⁸_____ (plan) to return to England in the year 2009.

4 Match the words (1–6) with the definitions (a–f).

1 unique
2 range
3 frozen
4 violation
5 border
6 village

a changed to ice, very cold
b the frontier between two countries
c a small town
d the only one of its kind
e breaking a rule or regulation
f a group of mountains, e.g. the Himalayas

listening bank

03 A summer job

You are going to listen to a conversation between Dave and Monica, who are university students in the UK, discussing their summer holidays. Listen to the recording as many times as you need to and try to answer the questions. The recording is on the MultiROM at the back of this Student's Book.

1 Complete Dave's email to Monica about his experiences in Spain with the correct word from the list below.

Australia   Barcelona   August   taxi   Jordi
Trixi   forty   money   French   couple

Dear Monica,

I have just got back from Spain. I had a great time. I went to
1 _____ for the summer. I went to see a friend called
2 _____ who invited me to spend a 3 _____ of
weeks there. I wanted to stay all the summer so I decided to
get a job because I didn't have enough 4 _____ . I
found a job with a company called 5 _____ . I drove a
special 6 _____ which was really a bicycle designed
for two passengers. Every day I rode about 7 _____
kilometres. I liked the job a lot. I now speak Spanish and
8 _____ much better. I stayed there until the end of
9 _____ . I made friends with a lot of people including
a girl called Jessica from 10 _____ .

See you soon

Dave

---

2 Mark the sentences true (T) or false (F).

1 Jordi helped Dave to get the job with Trixi. _____

2 Jordi is a student like Dave. _____

3 Dave's first job was in a bar. _____

4 The taxi uses an electric motor all the time. _____

5 Dave stayed in Jordi's house all summer. _____

6 Dave thinks he rode about 1,500 kilometres. _____

3 Put the questions from the dialogue in the correct order. Then listen again to check your answers.

1 did / have / summer / a / good / you?

2 have / been / what / you / doing / so?

3 by / what / mean / you / riding / do / taxi / a?

4 so / you / have / what / to / been / up?

5 Erasmus / he / here / come / didn't / with?

6 are / going / taxis / to / me / tell / when / the / you / about?

4 Match the phrases (1–7) with the definitions (a–g).

1 You look really fit!

2 I'm coming to that!

3 a cycle path

4 the sightseeing areas in the centre

5 I earned enough to live on.

6 tips from the tourists

7 I got on really well with them.

a a special road only for people on bicycles

b popular places of interest for tourists

c money you give a waiter, taxi driver, etc.

d We were good friends.

e You have a good, healthy appearance.

f I will explain in a minute.

g sufficient money for your needs

listening bank

Flying high

You are going to listen to an interview with Ildikó Czigány, Hungary's first female captain, flying passengers for the national airline, Malév. Listen to the recording as many times as you need to and try to answer the questions. The recording is on the MultiROM at the back of this Student's Book.

1 Listen and put the events below in chronological order.

_____ becoming a captain
_____ learning to fly
_____ studying music
_____ studying Forestry and Wildlife
_____ working in TV

2 Listen again and (circle) the best answer.

1 What has Ildikó Czigány done?
   a become a professional pilot
   b become an amateur pilot
   c become a fighter pilot

2 What did she study after school?
   a veterinary science
   b music
   c TV production

3 Why did Ildikó Czigány like her job in TV?
   a She worked the same hours every day.
   b She worked abroad, not in Budapest.
   c She travelled a lot and used her languages.

4 Why did she give up her job in TV?
   a The journeys from work to the flying club were too much for her.
   b She didn't like it.
   c She decided to become a waitress.

5 It was good to be an air hostess because
   a she had a lot of contact with the pilots.
   b she used the radio telephone system.
   c she liked working with the passengers.

6 Ildikó Czigány started flying when
   a she tried flying back from Paris.
   b a pilot told her about a club near Budapest.
   c a Russian showed her how to fly.

7 It was difficult to learn to fly because
   a it was difficult to travel in Hungary then.
   b she was too young.
   c she was female.

8 How long did it take her to become a passenger plane pilot?
   a four years
   b five years
   c nine years

9 What does a captain do that a first officer does not?
   a The captain flies the plane.
   b The captain gives all the instructions.
   c The captain is responsible for all the decisions that are made.

10 She does not fly bigger planes now because
   a she does not like long flights.
   b she has a lot of pets at home.
   c the smaller planes are easier.

Glossary

cockpit where a plane's pilot sits
glide to fly without using power, only the wind

Answer key

1 1 studying music
  2 working in TV
  3 learning to fly
  4 studying Forestry and Wildlife
  5 becoming a captain

2 1 a
  2 b
  3 c
  4 a
  5 a
  6 b
  7 c
  8 c
  9 c
  10 b

listening bank

Low-cost airlines

You are going to listen to a radio programme about low-cost air travel. Listen to the recording as many times as you need to and try to answer the questions. The recording is on the MultiROM at the back of this Student's Book.

1 Mark the sentences true (T) or false (F).

1 Low-cost airlines only fly to capital cities. _____

2 The Internet helps these companies to reduce their costs. _____

3 Tom always goes to Spain alone. _____

4 Margaret went to Amsterdam to see a football match. _____

5 She paid £67 for her return ticket to Amsterdam. _____

2 What do these numbers refer to? Listen to the recording again to check your answers.

1 1992 _____

2 17p _____

3 £40 _____

4 nearly £3 _____

3 Harriet explains how low-cost airlines can offer low prices. Tick (✓) which of the following reasons she mentions.

1 Their clients use the Internet to do everything. _____

2 They do not have many offices. _____

3 People have to reserve their tickets a long time before they fly. _____

4 They do not use expensive airports. _____

5 They only operate on popular routes. _____

6 They pay lower salaries to their staff. _____

4 Margaret did not enjoy her flight to Amsterdam. Put her sentences in the correct order 1–8. Listen to this part of the recording again to check your answers.

a _____ All my friends told me that I should fly with one of these low-cost companies.

b _____ I booked my tickets for a weekend trip to Amsterdam.

c _____ I prefer to pay a little more but to have better service.

d _____ The final price came to sixty-seven pounds.

e _____ The plane was full of all these football supporters.

f _____ Then I had to pay nearly three pounds for a cup of tea and a biscuit!

g _____ We were delayed by nearly two hours.

h _____ When I got to the airport there was a long queue of people waiting for the flight.

listening bank

Wind power

You are going to listen to an interview with an expert on wind power. Listen to the recording as many times as you need to and try to answer the questions. The recording is on the MultiROM at the back of this Student's Book.

Glossary

climate the type of weather a place has
hectare a unit for measuring an area of land = 10,000 square metres

1 Match the words (1–10) with the definitions (a–j).

1 energy
2 ideal
3 oil
4 planning permission
5 self-sufficient
6 solar
7 renewable
8 to store
9 wind
10 growth rate

a able to provide for yourself everything you need, without help from other people
b relating to the sun, or coming from the sun
c how quickly something increases
d something which can be used again
e electricity and other forms of power used to make things work
f to keep in a particular place
g a thick dark smooth liquid used for making petrol and other fuels
h air moved by natural forces
i of the best type, perfect
j the right to build something, given to you by someone in authority

2 Mark the sentences true (T) or false (F).

1 Wind energy was popular in the 1980s, because people did not want to depend on other sources of energy.
2 The new windmills provide energy that is used at a later date.
3 Other supplies of energy are limited, so wind power is an important alternative.
4 A wind turbine has four blades.
5 Large wind turbines can have a rotor diameter of up to ninety metres.
6 If there is enough wind, then the windmill can serve a family for about three years.
7 The best place to build windmills is on very hilly ground, inland.
8 The public complain about windmills harming their animals, and destroying their land.
9 The RSPB are totally in agreement with windmills.
10 Europe has not reached the 2010 targets yet.

wind
blade
wind turbine

grammar bank

Grammar terms

noun: a word that is the name of a thing, an idea, a place, or a person

adjective: a word that tells you more about a noun

verb: a word that shows something happens or exists

adverb: a word that adds more information to a verb or adjective

article: the words *a / an* and *the*

preposition: a word like *for, of, to, from*

The present

Present simple (*I walk*)

The present simple is used for general facts about the present, descriptions, habits, routines, and schedules.

> Moscow is the capital of Russia. (general fact)
> Their new operation seems very efficient. (description)
> I work in London three days a week. (routine)
> Our flight leaves at 10.45. (schedule)

The present simple is used for stative verbs. These are verbs used to describe ways of thinking, possession, and senses (*taste, hear, feel*, etc.).

> I think it's a great idea. (way of thinking)
> We have offices all over the country. (possession)
> Pastilla tastes sweet. (sense)

Present continuous (*I am walking*)

The present continuous is used to talk about actions at the time of speaking, and actions happening around now.

> She's talking to one of the designers at the moment.
> (time of speaking)
> We are looking for a supplier in the Far East.
> (happening around now)

It is used to talk about the future to refer to definite future arrangements.

> I'm flying to Peru tonight.

Present perfect (*I have walked*)

The present perfect is used for actions in the past which still have a connection to the present. It is also used for actions that have very recently finished. It may be used to report news.

> I've worked here for three months.
> (unfinished time period = time when working here)
> The air conditioning has stopped working.
> (stopped very recently)
> Some money has gone missing! (news)

The past

Past simple (*I walked*)

The past simple is used for actions that happened in finished time periods.

> We met at the meeting in Seoul last month.
> (finished time period = last month)
> I spoke to the suppliers yesterday.
> (finished time period = yesterday)

Past continuous (*I was walking*)

The past simple is the most common tense used for past actions. The past continuous is often used with the past simple to emphasize background information, and longer actions.

> We were travelling from Cairo to Dubai.
> (background information)
> I had a great idea while I was looking at the new layout.
> (shorter action = had a great idea, longer action = looking at the layout)

The future

Future simple (*I will walk*)

Will is used for general predictions about the future.

> Labour costs will increase over the next five years.

Will is often used in the present for immediate decisions and offers.

> I'll have to check those figures. (= decide immediately to check the figures)
> I'll go and get the post. (= offer to collect the post)

Going to future (*I am going to walk*)

Going to and *will* can often be used in the same way to make predictions.

> Labour costs are going to increase over the next five years.

Going to is used in predictions which are based on present evidence.

> We're going to have logistical problems, because the system has shut down.
> (present evidence = the system has shut down, prediction = have logistical problems)

Both *going to* and the present continuous are used to describe definite future arrangements.

> I'm going to fly to Peru tonight.

Future continuous (*I will be walking*)

We use the future continuous when we predict what will happen at a specified future time.

> I will be leaving at 7.00 p.m. today.

Like *going to* and the present continuous, the future continuous is used to talk about future plans and arrangements.

> We'll be arriving at 6.00 p.m. tomorrow.

Conditionals

First conditional (*If you walk, it will take ten minutes*)

The first conditional is used to describe something which could happen in the future and its result.

> If I attach the file to the email, you'll be able to open it.
> (something which could happen = attach file, result = open it)

Second conditional (*If I walked to work, it would take hours*)

The second conditional is used to describe something which is less likely to happen in the future and its result. It also describes something in the present or the future which is unrealistic.

> If I had the right software, I would design the book myself.
> (something which is less likely to happen = had the right software, result = design the book myself)

We can change the two parts of a conditional sentence around. In this case there is no comma between the two clauses.

> I would design the book myself if I had the right software.

If I were is used for giving advice.

> If I were you, I'd get here on time.

Passives

The passive is used for various reasons. It is made with the usual verb tense of *be* + past participle.

> She was headhunted by a rival company.
> (usual tense of *be* is past simple = was, past participle = headhunted)

We may use a passive when we do not know who did an action.

> My files have been moved! (= we don't know who moved the files)

We may use a passive when the person who did an action is not important to us.

> My brother has been promoted!
> (= the speaker is interested in his brother, not who promoted his brother)

We may use a passive to describe a process, such as the manufacture of a product.

> The cheque was issued in your name, and it was deposited on Friday last week.

In a passive sentence, if we want to include who did the action, we use *by*.

> My brother has been promoted by his new boss!
> (who did the action = his new boss)

Articles

The indefinite article (*a, an*)

Use *a / an* to talk about something for the first time.

> A new order has just come in. (= first mention of the new order)

The definite article (*the*)

Use *the* after mentioning something for the first time.

> Have you dispatched the order yet?

Use *the* when you expect the other person to know exactly what / who you are talking about.

> I've asked John to drive the van.

Use *the* when there is only one of something.

> The boss is out of the office today.

No article

General descriptions of uncountable nouns do not use an article.

> Unemployment is increasing rapidly.
> (uncountable noun = unemployment)

General descriptions of countable nouns do not use an article. The countable noun becomes plural.

> Women are more likely to work part-time than men.
> (plural countable nouns = women, men)

Countable and uncountable nouns

Nouns can be singular or plural, countable or uncountable.

> Singular: computer, book
> Plural: computers, books
> Uncountable: software, sugar, water

Some / any

Some is used with plural, countable nouns and uncountable nouns. *Some* is used in positive sentences, offers and requests, and questions where we expect the answer *yes*.

> I have some new keyboards for the computers.
> (countable nouns = keyboards, computers)
> I have some software to install on your computer.
> (uncountable noun = software)
> Do you want some coffee? (= expect the answer *yes*)

Any is used with uncountable nouns and plural countable nouns in negatives and questions.

> Do you have any new keyboards? (countable noun = keyboards)
> There isn't any new software. (uncountable noun = software)

Much / many

Use *much* with uncountable nouns and *many* with countable nouns.

> How much new software do we need to install?
> (uncountable noun = software)
> How many computers do we need to service?
> (countable noun = computers)

Much and *many* are not usually used in positive sentences. In positive sentences use *a lot of* or *lots of*, which can be used with countable and uncountable nouns.

> There is a lot of / lots of new software to install.
> There are a lot of / lots of computers to service.

Modal verbs

Modal verbs are auxiliary verbs that we use to show ability, obligation, or opinion. They include *can, could, may, might, should, have to, must*, and *need to*.

> We can put out a press release. (can = ability)
> We should contact the Minister. (should = opinion)
> We have to get a visa to visit Canada. (have to = obligation)

Modal verbs are followed by the bare infinitive (i.e. the infinitive without *to*).

> I could help him. (could = modal, help = bare infinitive)

grammar bank

Questions

In questions, an auxiliary verb, and sometimes also a question word, go before the subject and the main verb. Question words include *who, what, where, when, why,* and *how.*

> What is he doing?
> (what = question word, is = auxiliary verb, he = subject, doing = main verb)
> How do you know?
> (how = question word, do = auxiliary verb, you = subject, know = main verb)
> Has she done it yet?
> (has = auxiliary verb, she = subject, done = main verb)

When a question word is also the subject of a sentence, no auxiliary verb is used.

> What broke the machine?
> (what = question word and subject, broke = main verb, the machine = object)
> Who wants the book?
> (who = question word and subject, wants = main verb, the book = object)

Indirect questions

Reported questions change normal question word order.

> Do you know what he does?
> ~~Do you know what does he?~~
> Can you tell me who she is?
> ~~Can you tell me who is she?~~

Question tags

Question tags are used to ask for agreement or to check information. A question tag is made from the auxiliary verb from the first part of the sentence and a pronoun.

> You are not from the Prague office, are you?
> (are you = question tag, are = auxiliary, you = pronoun)

If you have a positive sentence, the tag is negative.

> You know Helena, don't you?
> (You know Helena = positive sentence, don't you = negative tag)

If you have a negative sentence, the tag is positive.

> You haven't been to the New York office, have you?
> (You haven't been to the New York office = negative sentence, have you = positive tag)

Comparatives

Comparatives are used to show the differences between things. Adjectives of one syllable form a comparative by adding -*er*.

> strong – stronger
> This CV is much stronger than the others.

Adjectives of two syllables ending in –*y* form a comparative by changing –*y* to –*i* and adding –*er*.

> easy – easier
> I think this project will be easier if we work together.

Other two syllable adjectives form a comparative by using *more*.

> boring – more boring
> That presentation was even more boring than his last one!

Adjectives with more than two syllables form a comparative by using *more*.

> complicated – more complicated
> The new system is more complicated than the old one.

Superlatives

Adjectives of one syllable form a superlative by adding –*est*.

> strong – strongest
> She's the strongest candidate.

Adjectives of two syllables ending in –*y* form a superlative by changing –*y* to –*i* and adding –*est*.

> easy – easiest
> That's the easiest way to do it.

Other two syllable adjectives form a superlative by using *most*.

> boring – most boring
> That was the most boring presentation I've ever heard.

Adjectives with more than two syllables form a superlative by using *most*.

> difficult – most difficult
> It was the most difficult job interview I've ever had.

listening script

1.1

1

Jordi Hey, Jenny! Good to see you again.

Jenny Jordi, hi. I didn't expect to see you here. How are you?

Jordi Fine, thanks. And you?

Jenny Not bad. Is Tim coming too?

Jordi No. He can't come.

Jenny That's a shame. Oh look, here's Asim. Hi there! Do you know each other? Jordi – this is Asim Khan. He's from Karachi.

Jordi Hi. Nice to meet you.

Asim Nice to meet you too. When did you get here?

Jenny About an hour ago. And you?

Asim I came early this morning … and this is Safina. She works here in Cairo. I'm sorry, what did you say your name was?

Jordi I'm Jordi. From Barcelona. Good to meet you. Jenny and I were on Gary's course in London last year. Have you met Gary?

Safina No, not yet. But I've heard a lot about him.

Jordi Well, let me introduce you. He's just over there… Er … Gary. Can I introduce you to Safina?

Gary Hi, Safina. How are you? Ah yes – you did the online designs. It's nice to put a face to the name at last!

Safina Pleased to meet you.

Gary Would you like something to drink?

Safina Thank you. Um, yes, an orange juice, please.

2

Jordi I'm afraid it's getting late. I really must go. The taxi's waiting outside.

Jenny OK. It was a great week, wasn't it?

Jordi Very good – especially the pyramids.

Jenny Yes. Don't forget to send me the photos.

Jordi No, I won't. Take care, Jenny. Bye.

Jenny Yes. Keep in touch and say hi to Tim from me.

Jordi Of course. See you then and goodbye, Safina.

Safina Goodbye, Jordi. Have a good journey. It was great to meet you.

Jordi Bye, everyone.

Safina So, Jenny, when are you leaving?

Jenny My flight is at six, so … not for a while.

Safina Well, please visit us here again one day … Gary!

Gary Safina, hi.

Safina I just wanted to say … Thanks for everything. It was a great course.

Gary Not at all! Thank you for telling us about the project. And are you in Dubai next month?

Safina Yes, for the regional team meeting.

Gary Well, I'll send you the schedule next week. See you then. All the best!

Safina I'll look forward to seeing you again. Goodbye.

2.1

Mike So the company's results are not good. But anyway, let's hear what the union has to say.

Maureen Shall I start, Pat?

Pat Yes, why not?

Maureen Now, last year, our pay rise was below inflation.

Pat Yes.

Maureen This year, we want a pay rise of inflation plus 2%. Inflation is at 3.2%, so we're talking about 5.2%.

Pat And how about a bonus? We talked about that last year.

Mike Vince, you're the manager. Do you think those extra costs will make our products more expensive than our competitors' products?

Vince Definitely. It will be good news for our competitors.

Mike Thank you, Vince. I'll tell you what, Pat, Maureen, I'll agree to a pay rise the same as inflation, but no more. That's my offer.

2.2

Maureen Now after thinking about it, Mike, sorry, but we don't think your offer of 3.2% is enough.

Mike There's no way we can pay 5.2%. We can't afford it. Now, I've asked Josie from Human Resources to come along. Would you like to say something, Josie?

Josie Thank you, Mike. Now, none of our competitors are agreeing to a 5.2% increase. In fact, they're cutting their costs. But why don't we look at Pat's idea of the bonus?

Maureen Go on.

Pat We're listening.

Josie OK, how about this: if we meet our sales targets for this year, then 10% of all profit will go directly into salaries.

Maureen Sorry, Josie, do you mean just one payment here?

Josie Yes. Exactly. A one-off payment.

Pat Hmm, that's not a bad idea.

Josie I think it's a great idea. Now would you like me to show you the sales predictions for this year?

Mike Yes, let's look at those in just a moment. Now, Maureen, Pat.

Maureen Yes, Mike?

Mike You understand that … we'll offer this bonus if you agree to a pay rise of 3.2%.

Maureen What about 4.2%?

Mike Sorry, that's out of the question. Absolutely impossible.

Pat We'll have to think about your offer. We'll talk again tomorrow.

3.1

1 In the office

John Hi Fran. Hey, do you want some help?

Fran No, it's fine thanks, John. It's just… well … where are the new books on Austria?

John They're in the other office. I'll just get them.

Fran OK. Thanks. I want to pack up all the boxes first, and then, I'll do the brochures, and after that I'll put the T-shirts and pens out.

2 At the car

Fran Oh dear. We've got so many things. Do you think there's room for everything?

John Yes, of course! Wait. Let me help. First of all, I'll put the back seat down. Then we can put these boxes in. OK?

Fran And the laptop?

John We can put it on top, here. Right? Now there's lots of space. See?

Fran And the posters?

John Don't worry. There's plenty of room. Leave it to me. I'll bring them down from the office afterwards.

3 Setting up the stand

John Oh hello, Fran. You're here early. Are you doing OK?

Fran Of course I am. There's just a lot to do, isn't there?

John Yes. Do you want a hand?

Fran No, no. It's fine.

John Well, why don't I empty the boxes?

Fran No really. I can do it myself. I'll do the boxes first, and then do the table.

John Come on. How can I help?

Fran It's all fine, I think.

John How about a coffee. Shall I get one for you?

Fran No. I haven't got time.

John Right. OK. Just one for me, then. Oh, and, Fran, very nice T-shirt, but it's back to front!

Fran Oh no! Thanks.

4 The end of the trade fair

John Well. Everyone's gone home, and all the freebies have gone!

Fran Yep. Oh, I'm so tired! Look! It's quite late already.

listening script

John Listen, can I get you a drink? There's a pub over the road.

Fran No, no. Not yet. I want to clear up these things. First I'll put all the books back in the boxes, and after that I'll …

John Fran! Not now. We can do it together later.

Fran Oh. All right then. Actually, a large beer would be great!

4.1

Dave I'd like to speak to Angela Ferrer please.

Angela Speaking.

Dave Oh, hello. This is Dave Jones and I'm phoning from London. I work for ALDI-LITE Ltd. and we have to…

Angela Excuse me, could you just spell your company name for me please?

Dave ALDI-LITE. That's A-L-D-I hyphen L-I-T-E. ALDI-LITE Ltd.

Angela And how can I help you, Mr Jones?

Dave My company is organizing a sales meeting in Amsterdam next month on the 27th and we need to reserve a large meeting room.

Angela Did you say the 27th?

Dave Yes.

Angela Let me see. How many people are coming to the meeting?

Dave About thirty.

Angela Excuse me, was that thirteen or thirty?

Dave Sorry. Thirty, three-oh. Around thirty to forty people.

Angela Well, the Maastricht room has a capacity for fifty people so that would be the best one for your meeting … and it's free on the 27th.

Dave Good. How much does it cost, please?

Angela Do you need the room for the whole day?

Dave No, just the morning, until lunchtime.

Angela The rate for the morning is … just a second … six hundred and twenty-five euros.

Dave Does that include tax, and all other costs?

Angela Yes, yes, it does.

Dave Great, and, er… is it possible to organize a coffee break, at about 11.00?

Angela Yes, that's no problem. We charge three euros per person.

Dave Three euros, good. And would it be possible to have lunch at the hotel?

Angela Yes, the standard menu is twenty-seven euros per person.

Dave Sorry, how much did you say?

Angela Twenty-seven euros.

Dave Oh, and just one other thing – we need a projector and screen for the meeting. Is this possible?

Angela Do you mean a projector for transparencies or for a computer?

Dave A computer projector, please.

Angela That's not a problem. It's included in the fee for the room.

Dave Well, I think that's everything – oh, could you give me your email address please?

Angela Yes of course, the address is aferrer@apeldoornhotel.nl.

Dave Sorry, could you repeat that, please?

Angela Yes. I'll spell it for you, if you like: a-f-e-r-r-e-r at a-p-e-l-d-o-o-r-n-h-o-t-e-l dot n-l. aferrer at apeldoornhotel all one word dot n-l. When can you confirm the reservation, please?

Dave Probably tomorrow. I'll send you an email. Well, thank you very much.

6.1

Gina How was your trip to Paris?

Simon OK, I guess.

Gina Just OK? I'd love to go to Paris for work!

Simon Well, travelling for work sounds fun, but it can be boring. Or annoying!

Mark Why annoying?

Simon Um, well, if things go wrong, for example, if your flight's overbooked and you have to wait a long time for the next one…

Gina I don't understand – what do you mean overbooked?

Mark Oh – airline companies always sell too many tickets for a flight. There are more passengers than seats!

Gina Really?

Simon Mmm that's right. It's a lot more common than people think. They do it because they know that some people will cancel their flight or miss it. If they didn't overbook the flight, they'd take off with empty seats and lose money.

Gina Oh! I never knew that.

6.2

Simon OK, well, I was in London a few years ago on a business trip, and I was flying back home to the States from Heathrow, and I could see that the plane was going to be really full. I mean, people were lining up for miles.

Mark Overbooking, right?

Simon Exactly, and I could see these two ground staff.

Gina Oh yes.

Simon They were coming down the line, asking everybody at check-in a question. Can you guess what it was?

Gina No.

Mark Me neither.

Simon They were asking everybody, very politely 'Because this flight to New York is overbooked, would you mind flying tomorrow instead of today?'

Mark And what did you say?

Simon Well, I could see that there were families on vacation, there were sports teams and so on, and they probably had a tighter schedule than me. And I was going home, so a day earlier, a day later, what the heck.

Gina And that's what you told them?

Simon No, I said: 'It would be very inconvenient for me not to take this flight today, but if you don't find anyone, come back and talk to me again…'

6.3

Simon And guess what? They couldn't find anyone else: the families couldn't wait a day, neither could the sports teams.

Gina But you were more flexible?

Simon I knew if they came back, the situation would be worse. So I told them: 'As I said before, it's not convenient for me to miss this flight, but you can put me on tomorrow's flight if you upgrade my seat to first class.'

Gina Hey, that was good! You –

Simon Hang on, I'm not finished yet. 'You upgrade my seat to first class, give me a four-star hotel in London tonight, and £150 in cash'.

Mark Wow! First class, a four-star hotel, and £150!

Gina And did they?

Simon What do you think? They agreed immediately.

Mark I think you're smarter than I am, Simon.

Simon Just more experienced at travelling, Mark.

Gina And then?

Simon Well, I phoned home and told my wife I'd be getting home one day later than planned.

Gina Did she mind?

Simon Mind? Hey, she met me at the airport with her lawyer!

7.1

Melissa So, your first day! How are you getting on? Are we making you work too hard?

Susan No, no, everything's fine. The first day's always the worst!

Melissa OK. If you're my new PA, you have to know what I do. Right?

Susan Yes, of course.

Melissa Well. I always get to the office at eight. It's nice and quiet then. Is that a problem for you?

Susan   No, no problem. What should I do first?

Melissa   Please always check my email and letters first. We usually have a short meeting at about nine o'clock.

Susan   Nine o'clock. OK. Is that every day?

Melissa   If I'm in the office, that is. I'm always here on Mondays and Fridays. We plan my day, arrange my appointments, and organize my visits.

Susan   So you usually visit the clients on Tuesdays, Wednesdays, and Thursdays?

Melissa   That's right. I like to have my meetings with clients in the mornings if possible. They never visit me. I always have to go to them. Oh! I'm not here until nine on Wednesdays.

Susan   Do you have a meeting then?

Melissa   No, I go to the gym every Wednesday at seven in the morning and I get here around nine.

Susan   I see. Do you have any weekly or monthly meetings here?

Melissa   Yes. We have a planning meeting every Friday morning. Then we have the big sales meeting on the second Monday of each month. Can you use PowerPoint?

Susan   Yes. I used it a lot in my last job.

Melissa   Good, because I have to do a lot of presentations in my work.

Susan   How often?

Melissa   About three or four times a month.

Susan   Do you often go abroad?

Melissa   Not very often. I go to Paris three or four times a year – we have a big client there. I probably go abroad six or seven times a year, usually for conferences, but never for very long. You arrange all the tickets and reservations. And when I'm out of the office you supervise things for me.

Susan   The office closes at six, is that right?

Melissa   Yeah, but I'm flexible about that! We sometimes work later, but then you can usually finish work early the next day.

7.2

Cathy   So Susan, how's your first day going?

Susan   OK, I think. I'm working for Melissa Harris. Do you know her?

Cathy   Oh Melissa, the sales manager. Well, you're going to be busy!

Susan   Yes, I think so. Where shall we sit?

Cathy   How about over there, near the window?

…

Cathy   Where are you from, Susan?

Susan   I was born in Birmingham but I moved to London about three years ago.

Cathy   Did you move here for the job?

Susan   Yes, but not for this one. I worked for a different company before.

Cathy   Do you like living here?

Susan   Yes, there are a lot of things to do.

Cathy   And what do you do in your spare time?

Susan   I like to do some sport. I run a little.

Cathy   How often do you do that?

Susan   Two or three times a week. At the weekend, I like to stay home and relax.

Cathy   Do you visit your family often?

Susan   Yes, I go back home about once a month and stay with them for a couple of days. What about you? Does your family live in London?

Cathy   No, my mother and sister live in Tenerife.

Susan   Tenerife! That's nice. Do you ever go and visit them?

Cathy   Yes, twice a year. Once in winter and then again in September or October. Do you want some coffee?

Susan   Yes, please, but let me.

Cathy   Don't worry. I'll get it.

8.1

José   Suzanne, let me get you a glass of Madeira wine.

Suzanne   Oh, thanks. That'll help me relax!

José   Here you are.

Suzanne   Thank you. Maybe first you can tell me who else is from Funchal.

José   Of course. Well, the branch manager here is Paulo Rodrigues. He's very open and friendly. You'd like him. He's the one over there, talking to the woman in the pink top.

Suzanne   Uh-huh. By the table?

José   Yes, that's right. And next to him there's a man with a moustache. In light brown trousers. He's quite well-built. Well he's the business development manager here. He's quiet and rather shy, but we get on very well.

Suzanne   And what about that man over there? The one with glasses. He looks very confident!

José   The one with the waistcoat? Yes, he's from Vienna. He's the

Director for Austria. We were chatting earlier. He's got a great sense of humour.

Suzanne   By the way, do you know who's here from Paris? I'd like to talk to the French manager, Henri Joli. He sent me those new brochures that head office produced, you know, the ones about VIP banking services. What's he like?

José   Ah, yes, Henri. He can be a bit serious and distant at times, and he's usually not very sociable, but when you get to know him, actually, he's good fun. I think you'd like him. Do you see the lady in black with high-heels? Well, she's talking to Henri. He's the one in jeans and trainers. Wearing a tie.

Suzanne   Right. Yes, I see. He seems much younger than I thought! And who's this guy over here? He's tall and thin, and rather smart. Do you know him?

José   Yes. Wearing a black pullover.

Suzanne   Uh-huh. He looks quite nice.

José   I think that's Antonio, from Italy. Anyway, before I introduce you to all these people, perhaps you'd like another drink, and maybe some of those cheese biscuits.

9.1

Tom   Good morning , good morning, everybody. Now can I have your attention, please? Thank you! Now I've just received our new working conditions for this year and I'd like to explain the important changes. OK. First the good news! The working week is now thirty-seven hours. So not thirty-nine but thirty-seven.

Workers   Great! Terrific! Good.

Tom   Yes. I'm sure there are no objections to that! This means that the new working day is as follows. We start at nine o'clock in the morning, that stays the same, but we finish work at half past five in the afternoon. That's Monday to Thursday, OK? Half past five. Everyone got that? Now on Fridays we start work at nine o'clock as usual but I'm very happy to say that the new time to finish work on Friday afternoon is three o'clock, not five o'clock as before.

Workers   Fantastic! Great!

Tom   OK? Everyone happy?

Workers   Yes! Sure.

Tom   But is one condition. If we finish at three on Fridays, the company doesn't think it is necessary to have a lunch break on that day.

Workers   What! No!

listening script

Tom So there's no lunch break on Fridays. We work from nine to three. We do finish at three, not five, remember. And, from Monday to Thursday the company want to reduce the lunch break from one hour to three quarters of an hour. That's to say from a quarter past one to two o'clock.

Worker 1 Only forty-five minutes!

Tom I know, I know, forty-five minutes is a bit short, but I think you can see the advantages.

9.2

Tom I know, I know, forty-five minutes is a bit short, but I think you can see the advantages. Now, can I go on to tell you about holidays? Well, the holidays at Christmas are the same, but we have one extra day at Easter.

Workers Good. Great.

Tom So that's three days not two.

Worker 2 What about the summer?

Tom We have the same number of days, twenty holiday days, but we now have to take the complete twenty days in July or August. Is that clear?

Worker 1 You said in July or August. What about September? Last year some of us took our holidays in September.

Tom I'm sorry but you can only take holidays in the summer in July or in August. These new conditions start on January 1st next year. Are there any questions?

Worker 2 Did you say we have one extra day at Christmas?

Tom No. We have one extra day at Easter, not Christmas.

Worker 3 What about the coffee break? Is that the same as before?

Tom Yes, you can take twenty minutes for coffee between 10.00 and 12.00 in the morning. Now do you want me to go over the changes again?

Workers Yes, please.

Tom OK, so the new working week is …

10.1

Sophie Good evening, could I speak to Leonard Wareham?

Mr Wareham Speaking.

Sophie Good evening, Mr Wareham. My name is Sophie from Portugal Homes. Is this a good time to call?

Mr Wareham Er … what about?

Sophie Well, Mr Wareham, how does the idea of free holidays for the rest of your life sound?

Mr Wareham Too good to be true?

Sophie Holidays in the Algarve area of Portugal…

Mrs Wareham Who is it, Leonard?

Mr Wareham Somebody about timeshares in Portugal. Excuse me, but I'm not interested.

Sophie But, Mr Wareham, this is a fantastic opportunity …

Mrs Wareham Leonard!

Mr Wareham Sorry, but I have to go.

Sophie Perhaps I could phone you later … Oh!

10.2

Isabel Can I start? First some background information. This campaign was for Portugal Homes. They contacted us in May last year about a new campaign for a development in the Algarve. We visited the client in their offices and had three meetings about the campaign. Er… OK… We then presented our proposal in June. We began to prepare the advertising, and for the next two months, we worked on the publicity. The advertising campaign was from September to November. And… um… we prepared a list of possible clients and telephoned them. A call centre did this cold calling for us. Portugal Homes did the first Sales Evening in January. A sales evening is when a group of twenty to forty clients meet a salesperson in a hotel for a presentation and sales talk. OK. I'm sorry if that's a lot of information in a very short time. We now have thirty minutes for your questions.

10.3

Isabel OK. I'm sorry if that's a lot of information in a very short time. We now have thirty minutes for your questions.

Voice 1 Did you have to change the budget?

Isabel Only once. The client decided to have more advertising on TV in December. They had to pay for this, of course.

Voice 1 Did you finish the project on time?

Isabel Just! We had to finish the campaign for the deadline in December.

Voice 2 And how many people did you call?

Isabel The call centre made 30,000 calls in October and November.

Voice 2 And how many people came to the sales evenings?

Isabel Well the sales evenings haven't finished. The sales manager of Portugal Homes has said that more than 5,000 people have been to the evenings so far.

Voice 2 Is the client happy with the results?

Isabel Yes, they are. Sales have increased by 23%. They have sold more than 350 holiday homes since January this year.

Voice 3 Have you finished your work with the client?

Isabel Not completely.

Voice 3 And the TV advertising?

Isabel No. That finished in November.

11.1

David Hello, John. How was your trip to Malta?

John Hi, David. Good. I saw several premises last week but they were all too small or too far or too expensive… Except one, that is.

David Yes? What were they like?

John Well, to tell you the truth, they're perfect for us. Around 250 square metres, brand new building, good parking facilities, and next to the main marina.

David Where are they exactly?

John In a completely new office complex – the Valletta Business Centre. It's a very nice place.

David They sound perfect. What's the problem?

John We can't rent them. They're for sale. We have to buy them.

David And how much are they asking?

John Just under €300,000: 270,000, to be exact.

David €270,000! That's ridiculous!

John That's what I thought, at first, but I went to see them and they are perfect! I made some calculations and …

David You're not going to tell me that you think we should buy them. I mean, where are we going to get the capital from?

John Well, I'm not a hundred percent sure but … I think it's a good opportunity.

David Now look, John, 270,000 …

11.2

David OK. John. Tell me where we are going to find €270,000.

John OK. Our first plan was to rent offices, right?

David Right.

John And we were thinking of a monthly rent in the region of six to seven thousand euros. Probably with a five-year contract?

David Yes, but a monthly rent, not buying.

John OK. Just a moment. And we agreed on a budget of €100,000 for possible building and decoration costs. From our own reserves, right?

David Yes.

John Well, these offices are brand new. We can save the €100,000. We don't need to spend our money on building work or decoration. We can just move in and start. And if we rent offices, we will have to pay a three-month deposit when we sign the contract. That's at least €20,000.

David OK. That's €120,000. Where's the rest of the money going to come from?

John The new offices cost €270,000. If we can invest 120,000 of our own money that only leaves €150,000.

David Only?

John Yes, but I'm sure the bank will give us a loan for the rest of the capital. We could borrow the money from the bank. Buying our own offices would be a good investment for the future. Property in Malta is increasing in price by over 15% a year at the moment. This is a good investment, believe me!

David Have you spoken to the bank about this?

John No, I haven't. But I'm sure the bank will lend us the money. We can get a seven- or a ten-year loan at about 8.75% annual interest.

David 8.75%?

John Yes. Listen, David. Why don't you come with me on my next trip to Valletta to see the new offices? If you like them, you can make an appointment with the bank to talk about a possible loan.

David OK. I'm interested but I'm not convinced. I'll speak to the bank but I'm not promising anything. I'll phone the bank now.

John Thanks, David.

12.1

1

Mark Diana?

Diana Yes?

Mark Hello, Mark here. This MTC project is so complicated! The, ah, automated test lines: can you bring me up to date on them? Are they going to be finished as planned?

Diana Well, we hoped to be able to finish the installation stage this month. But we're behind schedule.

Mark Are we?

Diana Yes. We're behind schedule by about … three weeks.

Mark Three weeks! I didn't know.

Diana We have a delay in the delivery of the machines from Italy. It's very new technology.

2

Mark So, the machines arrived OK.

Diana Yes. It was only a two-week delay in the end. We expect to be back on schedule very soon. We are starting the trial phase now and the machines look good.

Mark When will the centre be fully operational?

Diana We are going to be able to start the final stage, the production phase, in a week. They work so well that we expect to be able to save between 55 and 70% of the present costs of testing.

Mark But that's great news. So in one month, we'll be able to test new products twenty-four hours a day, 365 days a year.

Diana Yes. And these machines are great, Mark.

13.1

Tony Tony Ladbrook speaking.

Isabel Hello Tony. It's Isabel here. Have you got a moment?

Tony Yes, of course. Did you have a good weekend?

Isabel Oh, not very good. I was working!

Tony All weekend?

Isabel Yes, I was finishing the offer for the Italian contract. You know. The one for Italia Tours? I emailed it to them this morning. I hope we get the contract – it's very big – but I'm worried if they accept.

Tony You're worried?

Isabel Yes. We don't have enough staff. We simply haven't got enough people. You know how busy we are now.

Tony When will you get an answer from them?

Isabel They promised to give me a decision on Thursday. Can we meet on Friday and talk about it?

Tony Yes, sure. We can meet at ten o'clock in my office, and don't worry! We can recruit more staff if necessary. Let's wait and see.

Isabel OK. See you on Friday. Bye.

Tony Bye!

13.2

Tony Congratulations about the Italia Tours contract! That's great news.

Isabel Thank you, but we need to recruit some more people – and quickly.

Tony What staff do you think you need?

Isabel Well, I think I need a team of three people who can work on this contract. We should take on one admin person who can help in the office. We can get someone from an agency. A temporary secretary with a six-month contract. If possible, we need a person that speaks Italian well.

Tony OK. A temporary secretary. You said we needed a team of three people. The other two?

Isabel I think we should recruit a new accounts manager that can work on the Italia Tours job and help with the other work we have at the moment.

Tony What do you think? Should we look for someone full-time or not?

Isabel Yes, I think so. Someone who has three or four years' experience.

Tony OK. And the other person?

Isabel We need a graphic designer. Someone who's creative and who can produce results under pressure.

Tony Someone new? From outside the company?

Isabel No, I don't think so. I think we have the right person working for us now. I was thinking about Nicole. Do you know her?

13.3

Isabel I was thinking about Nicole. Do you know her?

Tony No, I don't think so. What does she look like?

Isabel She's French. She's quite tall. Long, dark hair. In her late twenties. She's been with us for five months.

Tony Only five months? She's not very experienced.

Isabel True, but I think she's had other jobs before in France. She's hard-working. She's very creative and imaginative, and she learns quickly.

Tony Right.

Isabel And she's completely dependable. When I worked with her before, she was the person who made our project work.

Tony So she's pretty efficient?

Isabel Yes. She, er … came to us on a six-month contract to help in the design department. Perhaps we could renew her contract for another six months.

Tony You'd recommend her?

Isabel Yes. I would.

Tony OK … Could I ask you a favour?

Isabel Yes, sure.

Tony Could you write me a short job description of the designer's job for the interview?

Isabel OK. I'll email it to you this afternoon.

14.1

Mike How did the McKinley campaign go?

Jane Oh, the McKinley campaign. We had a lot of problems with that client.

Mike Oh yes? Why?

Jane Well, they changed something every week. Every time they phoned, I knew they were going to change something. Did you know that they had three

listening **script**

different names? It was going to be *Kiwi Juice*. Then it was going to be *Kiwi Quick*. Finally they decided on *Kiwi Kool*.

Mike   Some clients are like that!

Jane   Yes, they were very difficult to work with.

Mike   But you finished?

Jane   Yes, we finished the campaign all right, but it was hard work.

Mike   Come on, tell me about it.

14.2

Mike   Come on, tell me about it.

Jane   Well. The first step was to meet the client in January. They said they were going to introduce a new fruit juice.

Mike   Kiwi Kool?

Jane   Yes, then they explained the sort of campaign they wanted. We were working on the proposal for two months and then we presented it to them at the end of February.

Mike   Did they like the proposal?

Jane   Yes, they did. We signed the contract in March … er … The next step was to prepare the publicity.

Mike   So far, so good.

Jane   Yes, but we were working on the publicity when they made the first big change.

Mike   What was that?

Jane   In the proposal, we were going to have a campaign on TV and radio, but at the beginning of April they said it was too expensive. So they cut the budget by 25%.

Mike   I see.

Jane   Yes. I was worried because our deadline was the end of May. But about the middle of April, they said they wanted another meeting about another 'minor' change.

Mike   What was it this time?

Jane   We were going to launch the product at shops and supermarkets.

Mike   And?

Jane   They said we had to concentrate on the supermarkets only. No shops!

Mike   But you started the campaign on time?

Jane   No, of course not! We only agreed on the final plan in May. We were going to start on the first of June but we weren't ready until the fifteenth.

Mike   Was the client pleased with the results?

Jane   I don't know! They were going to tell us the results at a meeting last week.

Mike   And?

Jane   They changed the date! We're going to see them next Monday now.

15.1

William   So, how's the new complex going?

Tony   Good. We're going to be on time. The work is going well – we'll be finishing the important building work at the end of December.

William   Good. That's on schedule.

Tony   And then we'll be starting the interior decoration, the work on the gardens, and the swimming pool area in January.

William   Do you think the hotel will be ready for December?

Tony   Yes. We'll be recruiting and training staff between June and August, and I expect we'll be taking our first reservations at the end of the summer, by September at the latest. The hotel will be operating at full capacity from the beginning of December, just in time for the winter season.

William   That's good news, Tony! Congratulations! You're doing a great job!

Tony   Thanks, William, but there's one thing we have to talk about.

William   Yes?

Tony   Yes. It's personal. I have finally made a decision about my retirement.

William   What have you decided?

Tony   Well, I'd like to work in the new hotel for the first year or so but I'll be retiring before the end of next year. I still haven't decided on an exact date.

William   Is that your final decision?

Tony   Yes it is, William. I'll be retiring next year.

William   Well, I'm sorry to hear that, Tony. But it's your decision. We should start looking for a new manager soon.

Tony   Why don't you appoint an assistant manager for June? We'll be employing new staff then, and it would be a good time to start.

William   That's a good idea. An assistant for June and, if you agree, he or she could take over from you when you leave.

Tony   Yes. That sounds sensible. We'll talk about it in London next month.

15.2

William   Hi Tony! Good to hear from you!

Tony   Hello, William. I'm afraid I've got some bad news.

William   Oh yes? You're over budget?

Tony   No, it's not a financial problem. But we're going to be behind schedule with the building work.

William   Yes? Something serious?

Tony   It could be. We can't start the work on the gardens and swimming pool area as we planned.

William   Why not?

Tony   There's a group of local people who are protesting about the plans. They say the swimming pool area is too near the beach.

William   Too near the beach? But the plans were accepted months ago.

Tony   Yes, but the local authorities say we have to stop for the moment. I'll be speaking to them next week about it.

William   What do you think will happen?

Tony   I don't know, but we won't be working on the gardens and swimming pools until the end of January. That's for sure.

William   Any other setbacks?

Tony   No, everything else is fine and on schedule. The architect says we could change …

William   No. No. We can't make any big changes now. Listen. When will you be seeing the people from the local authorities?

Tony   Next Tuesday at 11.00.

William   Would you like me to be there?

Tony   Thanks for the offer but I don't think that's necessary.

William   OK. Phone me as soon as you have any news.

Tony   I'll do that. Bye.

William   Bye. Too near the beach …?

16.1

Gavin   So did you have a good trip this time?

Charles   Yes, thanks. Excellent. But the city's changing so fast.

Gavin   OK. Well, let's go through each section. Where shall we start?

Charles   Right. Lahore. Have you got the copies I sent you there? Good. OK. Well, the first section on background, that's done. It won't change much at all, and the history stays the same. Under the sub-section 'getting about', I've added more details about maps and where to buy them.

Gavin   Ah ha. Will we have to change the city maps in the book too?

Charles   Yes, just a little. We need to point out some new cafés and restaurants. I'll talk to Ed about that. But I haven't done that yet.

Gavin   OK. Next. Tell me about the sightseeing section.

Charles   Well, we've still got all the main sights as before, you know, the mosque, the fort, the gardens, and so on, and I've already updated the opening times and prices of museums. They offer guides for the old city now, as well as to the Shalimar Gardens, so I've also included that. So, well, that section is ready too.

Gavin Good. But, er, what about the food markets?

Charles Well, they're in the next section, under shopping. And I've added some new CD shops and bookshops.

Gavin OK. Um, I hear there are three new shopping centres. Have you got those?

Charles Yes, I've already put them in. There are a few new shopping malls. But I've still got to add details about how to get there. I haven't done that yet. But I'll do it at the weekend.

Gavin OK. Let's move on now to the hotel section.

Charles Can we come back to that later?

Gavin OK, then. Tell me about the restaurant section.

Charles Well, er, there's still a lot of work to do in this section. I've already cut out the places that have closed. And I'm now checking times and prices of the old places. But a lot of local-style restaurants have opened up. My contact there, Louise, is doing some final checks for me. She said she'd get back to me by next Friday.

Gavin OK. But we haven't got long! We've only got until the end of the month. That's the deadline.

16.2

Gavin Well, before your trip we talked about the sports section, about making it more detailed. What have you got for that?

Charles Well, as you requested, I've included a special section on kite-flying. I've already got a general history of the sport, as well as a list of all the kite festivals, with a long list of dates and places.

Gavin Excellent. Kite-flying is competitive there, isn't it?

Charles Indeed. And it's actually quite dangerous. It's a very different game there. I've got the rules for that. I'd really like to include those too.

Gavin OK. Anything else?

Charles Well, I've also got some instructions with pictures for making kites. And I've also got a list of places where you can buy them.

Gavin That sounds really good. Thanks.

17.1

Judith OK. Let's start. This contract is really good news for us.

David Well, it's not all good news.

Judith Sorry?

David Well, about Friday. I'm afraid there's a problem with the samples. We haven't got enough of the hand creams in sample sizes. I can get you regular size

creams, but not giveaways. I'm sorry about that.

Judith OK. As long as we have enough samples of the other ranges it should be fine. And the soaps?

David We've got plenty – aloe, mint, whatever. But the thing is, we've had a problem with the lavender. The drivers were on strike and all the shipments were delayed. We're running low on stock now, but we should have it by Thursday in time for the event.

Judith Excellent, thanks. Now, who can go on Friday? Sue?

Sue Unfortunately, I can't. I'm going to a wedding.

Judith Oh. David?

David Well, … I've just booked tickets for the theatre. Sorry to let you down.

Judith Oh dear. Well, if either of you could change your plans, it would be a great help … Now, about the Christmas hampers. Sue, did you contact Tom? We need supplies of soaps by early September.

Sue Yes, he's just emailed. He can supply all the almond and mint soaps we need. And he mentioned the new aloe products. And we've got enough boxes of the olive ones too.

Judith Excellent. OK, that'll be fine. Thanks. Oh, I almost forgot, the best news is that Whittaker's have also offered to sell the lavender and olive range in their shop.

Sue Hey – you kept that quiet!

Judith Well, it's only for two years, but the contract is renewable.

David Well done, Judith. In that case, maybe I should go. I'll see if I can change my plans, but I can't promise anything …

19.1

1

Pat Great. OK, guys. Let's start. We haven't got enough time to talk about it all in detail, and I know you're all far too busy.

Anton Erm … if I may, um, Pat? Er, why exactly are we getting new uniforms? I mean, I don't understand. What's wrong with the old ones?

Pat OK, well, you see, management say that the old uniforms aren't smart enough. They should be more up-to-date.

Jim Yeah, it's a good idea to have a change.

Daniel Yes, sure. I'd opt for new uniforms.

Pat Anyhow, what do you think? Let's start with the shirts.

Jim OK. Well, we had a chat about these, and we decided that the

blue shirt looked best. We like the modern look, and it seems very practical.

Pat Right. But what about the short sleeves? Actually, I prefer the white one. I think it's really smart, and you'd all look great in it.

Daniel OK, but, er, are all those extra pockets necessary? There are far too many pockets.

Anton Exactly.

2

Pat OK. Well, let's try to make a decision about the trousers. Did you like these?

Daniel Yes, I think it's a good idea to have the big belt-loops. And I usually don't like pockets, but these cargo pockets are excellent.

Pat Jim?

Jim Yes, I'd choose those too.

Pat What do you think about the police-style trousers? I think they're perfect for a professional organization like ours.

Anton Well, I like the turn-ups, but not the zips. But perhaps they're not warm enough.

Daniel Yeah, I agree. I think you're right.

3

Pat OK. Well then, let's look quickly at the jackets. It's probably a question of zips or buttons. Which one did you like?

Jim I think the one with the buttons is best. And I like the one with the red under the collar.

Anton Yes, me too.

Pat So you don't like the navy blue jacket? The other one?

Daniel No, not much. In fact, I don't really like the cuffs. I hate elastic on sleeves.

Pat Oh. My preference is for the navy blue one with the zip. Well, it seems we don't really agree on any of these. Perhaps I should get another catalogue for you to see. But then maybe we'll have too much choice.

Jim Maybe. There aren't really enough options here. Um. When will we get the new uniforms? Is it soon?

Pat Well, if we use another company, we'll have to wait about twelve weeks, which is too long for us.

20.1

Robert So, let's take a look.

Maggie Interesting photos!

David Well, the most important thing is to show what Dubrovnik's like.

Robert Yes, but don't you think the photos should be at the top?

Maggie Yes, definitely. I couldn't agree more. Most people don't fully open the email.

business one : one   119
16.2–20.1

listening script

David OK. I'll move them up. Which three photos do you think are best?

Robert Well, they're all quite exciting. But the street artists one – I don't think it's a good idea at all.

Maggie Yes, it could be anywhere. What about a link on the email instead?

David You've got a point there. OK, so extra link to the summer festival. I'd like to include the seafood photo.

Robert I'm not sure about that one either.

Maggie But that's what people want on holiday. Open air restaurants, great food, you know …

David Indeed.

Robert Fair enough. I like the old city. I think it's ideal.

David Well, the history of Dubrovnik goes back a thousand years. I'm fascinated by it. OK. And finally, the sea with Dubrovnik?

Robert Absolutely.

Maggie I can't wait to go. I'm really excited about it all!

20.2

Robert OK, about the links. My feeling is that three is enough. All this text is a bit boring.

David Really? I'm afraid I don't really agree. But I can put villas and hotels together.

Robert Good idea. And this box with dates. The typeface is very big. Can you make the print smaller?

David Sorry? That's key information. You can't be serious!

Maggie Look, Robert. What matters is the destination, and price.

Robert OK. I suppose so. Look. Can we take a short break?

21.1

1

Elaine Good morning. Can I speak to Harriet, please?

Receptionist Yes. I'll put you through to Design.

2

Elaine Hello. I'd like to speak to Harriet, please.

Man This is Accounts. Harriet works in Design. Hold on a second.

3

Elaine Hello. Is that Harriet?

Harriet Yes, it is. Who's calling, please?

4

Elaine It's Elaine from Club Deluxe, Brussels.

Harriet Hello Elaine. Good to hear from you.

21.2

Elaine So Harriet … Do you think you'll be able to finish the flyer by the end of the month?

Harriet Yes. I think I can manage to do it by then.

Elaine Fine. I'll send you an email with the details, then.

Harriet Great. That'll be good. Do I have to sign a contract for the job?

Elaine Yes, you can come and sign the contract whenever you have time. Thanks for everything, Harriet.

Harriet Right. No problem.

Elaine Don't forget to call me if you've got any questions about my email.

Harriet OK. I could call you back when I've read it, if you want.

Elaine Right. We'll speak later then.

Harriet OK. I'll call you some time after 5.00.

Elaine Fine. I should be here.

Harriet Great. Bye, then.

Elaine Great. Bye, then.

Harriet Bye.

22.1

1

Announcer You have three messages. Message received at 11.40.

John Hi Ellis, John here. Just so you know, the train is leaving without me, which means I'm going to be really late. I'll get there as soon as I can, OK? Oh, I hate using voicemail. Sorry. Bye for now.

2

Rose Ellis, it's Rose. Just to tell you I'm on my way, but the traffic on the motorway isn't moving and it's 12.15 already. I don't like going through the city centre, but I think it's the best way. Just so you know I'll be there at about 12.40, all right? See you in a bit.

3

Sam Hello Ellis, this is Sam. I'm calling to see if you have any ideas where I can park because I'm not having a lot of luck here and it's 12.25 already! I don't understand what the problem is today, and I don't really want to leave the car on the pavement. Hopefully, I'll speak to you in a moment.

23.1

Kiko Good morning. On Spot Media.

Robert Oh, hello Kiko. It's … from Interview magazine.

Kiko I'm sorry, who's calling? Can you repeat your name, please?

Robert Yes, it's Robert Phillips from Interview magazine.

Kiko I'm very sorry, I still didn't catch your name. Could you say it again, please?

Robert Kiko, it's Robert. From Interview.

Kiko Oh yes, Robert. Of course. How are you?

Robert A bit busy, but apart from that …

Kiko Excuse me a moment, Robert, I've got another call.

…

Kiko Robert. Sorry about that. What can I do for you?

Robert Don't worry, Kiko. Can I have extension…

Kiko Robert? I'm afraid I can't hear you. Robert?

…

Kiko On Spot Media.

Robert It's me, Robert, again.

Kiko Oh, I'm sorry about that, Robert. I think we got cut off. Who did you want to speak to?

Robert Can you put me through to Yuichiro on extension 3390, please?

Kiko Can I have the number again, please?

Robert Yes, it's 3390.

Kiko Thanks. I'll put you straight through.

23.2

1

Caller I'd like to speak to Matti, please.

Receptionist I'm sorry, there isn't a Matti in this office.

2

Caller Ich möchte bitte mit Claudia sprechen.

Receptionist I'm afraid I don't understand. Do you speak English?

3

Caller Oh hello. It's Mehmet here.

Receptionist I'm sorry, who's calling? Can you repeat your name, please?

4

Caller It's about the project.

Receptionist Excuse me a moment, Mehmet, I've got another call.

5

Caller Hello, it's Mehmet again. We were speaking a minute ago.

Receptionist Oh, I'm sorry about that, Mehmet. I think we got cut off.

6

Caller I wanted to talk to Stuart about the JW111.

Receptionist I'm sorry. I'm not sure I understand.

24.1

Gerda Animalia Nature Theme Park. Can I help you?

Anne Hello. Is that Gerda Honne?

Gerda Yes, this is Gerda.

Anne It's Anne Kechel from Graphic Studies Group. We were talking last week about holding our anniversary party in Animalia.

Gerda Oh yes. We spoke last Thursday, didn't we? Would you like to make a booking?

Anne Well, we're extremely interested, but I wanted to ask you a few questions before we make our final decision.

Gerda OK. Go ahead.

Anne Well, you mentioned a tour of the park when we spoke. How long do you think the tour will take?

Gerda Probably about an hour and a half. Does that sound OK?

Anne That should be fine. But we're a bit worried about what will happen when we finish dinner.

Gerda Oh, you mean you want some sort of after-dinner entertainment?

Anne Yes. Have you got any ideas? Only we didn't think about this last week. Could we have somewhere a bit exotic to have a drink and dance, or somewhere more comfortable, where we can just sit and chat?

Gerda How about some dancing on Antarctic Island? It's usually really popular with our business clients, and we have a very good DJ, from er … Puerto Rico.

Anne That sounds really great. Perfect.

Gerda Good. Anything else?

Anne Yes. The price you sent me is per person, which is going to be a bit expensive for us. I was wondering if you could offer us a discount for a group booking.

Gerda Well, it depends on how many people there will be.

Anne About 400, I think.

Gerda I'm sure we can come to an agreement on a discount.

Anne Good. So, if you send me an email covering everything we've talked about, I'll get back to you next week with our decision, OK?

Gerda I'll send it right now. We'll speak next week, then. Thanks for calling.

Anne OK. Goodbye.

Gerda Bye.

25.1

1

Cathy Hello. Could I speak to Lars Johannsen, please?

Receptionist I'm afraid he's not at his desk right now. Can I take a message?

Cathy Yes, could you ask him to call me back, please? It's Cathy Lamble from Toronto. I'd like to arrange a meeting for next month.

Receptionist Could you give me your number, please?

Cathy Yes, it's 01 5487 29445.

2

Jean-Pierre Good morning. I'd like to speak to Gavan Bix, please.

Receptionist Who's calling, please?

Jean-Pierre It's Jean-Pierre Gauvain from Paris.

Receptionist I'm afraid he's talking on another line.

Jean-Pierre Can you give him a message for me, then?

Receptionist Yes, certainly.

Jean-Pierre Could you tell him I called and ask him if he agrees with a 3% price rise on all our products from January?

Receptionist Of course.

3

Caller Hi, is Rachel there?

Receptionist No, sorry, she must be at lunch. Shall I leave her a message?

Caller No, I'll call back in about three quarters of an hour.

Receptionist OK.

4

Jean Good afternoon. I'd like to speak to the manager, please.

Receptionist I'm afraid he's in a meeting. Who shall I say called?

Jean It's Jean Tan. You've sent us a bill for $369.50 and it can't be right. Please tell him to call me back urgently.

26.1

1 I'm having lunch at the moment. Call me back in an hour, OK?

2 No, I've got plenty of time. I'm just walking to the bus stop.

3 No, you're not disturbing me. I'm on my way home.

4 Ron, I'm talking to a client. I'll call you right back.

5 No, it's all right, I don't mind. I'm just watching the news.

6 Can't talk right now. I'm driving. We'll speak later, OK?

26.2

1 I'm terribly sorry, but I'm just getting on a plane. Would you mind calling me back this afternoon?

2 No problem, the meeting is just finishing. How can I help you?

27.1

1 Could you give me your number, please?

2 Hello. Is that Yvonne?

3 We'll speak later, then.

4 I'll send you an email with the details, then.

5 I'm sorry. Can you repeat your name, please?

6 Would you like to make a booking?

7 Have we spoken before?

8 Good morning. Can I speak to David, please?

9 Can you talk right now?

10 I'm afraid I can't hear you.

29.1

Marisa Hi David, I've looked at your text and there are a couple of changes.

David Oh, yes, I'll just get it back on screen … OK.

Marisa Now, the first sentence is good. I like that 'on behalf of'. In the second sentence, that beginning is too, erm, … abrupt. Let's change it to 'We would like to know if you are interested in, blah, blah, blah'.

David 'We would like to know if you are interested in', etc.

Marisa Next sentence: 'info' is too informal – put 'information'. OK?

David Yes.

Marisa Next sentence: 'can you' is a bit informal. Change it to: 'Would it be possible to blah, blah'. OK, David?

David 'Would it be possible for you …'

Marisa No, no, keep it simple. 'Would it be possible to.'

David Is that everything?

Marisa Just a sec, erm … the next two sentences are fine, fine. That 'would like to know your feelings' is nice – like that. And the last sentence is OK too. Right, you can send it.

David Thanks, bye.

Marisa Bye.

30.1

Dr Abbas Yes, yes, your product looks quite interesting, Mrs Hanhisalo. This High Pressure Liquid Chromatographer–

Mrs Hanhisalo The HPLC, yes.

Dr Abbas This HPLC could help our hospital in Dhahran to speed up the analyses. They're very slow at present. And this could be the solution. I'd like to follow this up.

Mrs Hanhisalo Thank you, Dr Abbas. Would you like to see how it works?

Dr Abbas I would like that very much, but I'm afraid I don't have time right now. Another time perhaps.

Mrs Hanhisalo Oh, that's a pity. Well, please take my card and get in touch if you think you might be interested.

listening script

Dr Abbas Thank you. Let me give you my card too. It's been nice talking to you.

1

Danilo Excuse me. I'm afraid I can't find my suitcase.

Woman Oh dear. Can you tell me which flight you were on, please?

Danilo Yes. I took Flight 357 to Atlanta and then Flight 55 to Tokyo.

Woman OK. And could you tell me what your name is, please?

Danilo Yes, it's Danilo da Sousa.

Woman Thank you. Now, your suitcase. What does it look like?

Danilo It's a large, green, plastic suitcase with wheels.

Woman Can you tell me if it has your name on it?

Danilo Only the label from the airline.

Woman Do you have the baggage label they gave you in Rio?

Danilo Yes. Here it is.

Woman Thank you. Now, could you tell me where you're going to stay in Tokyo? We'll send your suitcase to you as soon as possible.

2

Danilo Excuse me. Could you tell me where the buses go from, please?

Man Yes. They leave from outside the terminal building.

Danilo Have you any idea how much it costs?

Man Well, it depends. Where do you want to go?

Danilo I want to go to the city centre. Do you know which number I need?

Man You can take the Airport Limousine Bus to the centre. It costs about 3,000 yen.

Danilo Oh dear. I haven't got any yen. Do you know where I can change some money?

Man Well … you could try the bank over there.

Danilo Good idea. Thank you so much for your help.

1

Reception Reception. How can I help you?

Mrs Alekseeva Hello. This is Mrs Alekseeva. I'm in room 501. I've got a problem. Well, it's about the balcony door. I opened it, and now I can't shut it. The door won't lock. The um, you know, it's the thingy, the …. um it's for opening and closing the door, you hold it, but doesn't lock. It doesn't do anything.

Reception The handle, you mean?

Mrs Alekseeva Yes, the handle. Yes, it turns, but that's all. Could you send someone up?

Reception I'll get someone to come and have a look at it straight away.

2

Reception Good afternoon. Reception.

Mrs Alekseeva Hello. This is Irena Alekseeva. I'm in room 501.

Reception Yes? What is it?

Mrs Alekseeva Well, it's my jacket. It's been in my suitcase and now it's very … it looks bad. It's very creased. I'd like, you know, something for pressing clothes. Have you got one?

Reception Right. You want an iron to press your clothes?

Mrs Alekseeva Oh, yes, that's right. An iron.

Reception Well, I'm afraid I can't lend you one. But I can have your jacket ironed for you.

Mrs Alekseeva Oh right. Can it be done now?

Reception If you hang it outside your room, I'll have it ironed, and returned to you within two hours.

3

Reception Reception. How can I help you?

Mrs Alekseeva Oh, hello again. This is Irena Alekseeva.

Reception Uh-huh. Yes?

Mrs Alekseeva Well, it's the bath. The water. I can't stop the water. I can't turn the, um, the what's it called? You know. You use it to turn off the water. It's got stuck. And the bath is getting very full.

Reception You mean the tap?

Mrs Alekseeva Yes, the tap.

Reception OK. I'll have it fixed. I'll speak to our plumber immediately.

Mrs. Alekseeva Oh, thank you.

Reception Oh, and Mrs Alekseeva, please take the plug out of the bath.

Mrs Alekseeva The plug?

Reception Yes, the plug. It's in the bath. You take it out to let the water go down.

Mrs Alekseeva Oh. Ah. Right. The plug. OK!

1

Hassan Are you ready to order?

Geoff Yes, please. Could you explain this, er, couscous and tajine?

Hassan Couscous is a very typical dish in this country. The basic ingredient is semolina.

Dede Excuse me, I don't know what semolina is.

Hassan Semolina? It's like wheat.

Dede Ah, wheat, yes.

Hassan Yes, and this is cooked in a casserole – it's a kind of slowly cooked mixture of vegetables and meat. There are many different kinds, with chicken, meatballs, lamb. Now, tajine is another sort of casserole of meat, vegetables, fruit, and nuts. It's cooked very slowly over a fire.

Geoff Is it made with semolina?

Hassan No. Just with vegetables and meat.

Geoff I see.

2

Dede Could you explain this one please – pastilla? Is it sweet?

Hassan Well, it's made with lots of thin pastry, made with flour and eggs. And with chicken inside, and nuts – almonds – and cinnamon, a semi-sweet spice, so it is a little bit sweet.

Dede OK, I'll have chicken couscous.

Geoff I can't make up my mind. It all sounds nice. What do you recommend?

Hassan The tajine kadide is very good, minced lamb with tomatoes. Our speciality.

Geoff I think I'll have that, the minced lamb kadide.

3

Hassan Now, would you like a first course?

Geoff What's the local dish?

Hassan Harira soup – it's a soup with a little meat.

Geoff That sounds good. I'll have the soup –

Dede And I'll try the salad.

Hassan And what would you like to drink: mint tea?

Dede Shall we have the mint tea, darling?

Geoff Yes, we'll have mint tea, please.

Waitress Are you ready to order?

Guest Yes, please. What is this, er, rigatoni?

Waitress It's a kind of pasta, like macaroni but bigger.

Guest I see, and what about this, this orecchiette tricolori? Is that a kind of pasta too?

Waitress Yes, it's also a sort of pasta, in the shape of an ear, a little ear.

Guest And tricolori means 'three colours', I suppose?

Waitress Yes, the three colours are made with vegetables and herbs.

Guest Hmm. It sounds good, but I think I'll have the rigatoni, please.

37.1

Walter Hi, Susana?

Susana Hello, Walter. Are you nearly here?

Walter No, I'm afraid I'm a bit lost.

Susana Oh dear. Where are you now?

Walter I'm somewhere near Colón. I got the airport bus, and I thought I could walk to your office from here.

Susana No, it's quite a long way from Colón, really.

Walter Oh no! And there are no taxis anywhere!

Susana It's OK. There's public transport. Er …

37.2

Walter So, how do I get to your office?

Susana Well, you've got two choices. You can either take the train to Nuevos Ministerios and walk up the road, or get on the number twenty-seven bus. What's the traffic like?

Walter Terrible. I think I'll get the train. Where do I go when I come out of the station?

Susana You need to turn left and go up Castellana Street.

Walter Is it far?

Susana No, it takes about ten minutes. You walk past the BBVA tower and a big department store, and then you go through the shopping centre.

Walter What do I do when I go into the shopping centre?

Susana First you need to go up the escalator. Then go out of the doors the other side and go past a café. You'll see some double doors on the right. Go through the doors and up the steps. Ask the guard at reception to call me when you get here.

Walter OK. I'll be there as soon as I can.

Susana All right. See you. Bye.

39.1

Robert Oh, hello, Angela.

Angela Hi Robert. Any plans for the weekend?

Robert Yes, I'm going to a wedding this Saturday in London.

Angela Oh yes? Who's getting married?

Robert A friend of the family. Peter, my younger brother, will be there.

Angela Peter. Is that your brother who works in Ireland?

Robert Yes, that's right. But he doesn't work in Ireland now. He has changed his job. He still works for the same company but he's working in the Ukraine now.

Angela The Ukraine!

Robert Yes. He's working on a new factory there at the moment.

Angela How long has he been there?

Robert Oh. Only a month. He is staying in a hotel in Kiev. The problem is that he is also working on a project in Odessa. He's always travelling between the two cities and it's a long way. He finds that very frustrating. But he loves Kiev. Anyway he has two more months there and then he's moving to a new project in Korea.

Angela Kiev! Korea! He gets around a lot! What exactly does he do?

Robert He's an engineer. He designs production lines. He travels a lot. He works for a British company but he never works in Britain. He's worked in Brazil, Canada, India, Taiwan, …

Angela What does he do in his spare time when he's in all these different countries?

Robert You don't get a lot of free time in his job! You just work. He told me that in the Ukraine he's going out a lot in the evenings because the people like to invite you to their homes. I think he reads a lot too when he's overseas.

Angela How often do you see him?

Robert Not often, I see him once or twice a year. I haven't seen him for nearly a year. I'm really looking forward to this Saturday. It'll be great to see him again.

Angela Yes, I'm sure. Well, back to work! Have a great weekend! Enjoy yourself!!

Robert Yes. Thanks. You too!

40.1

Ralf Something really strange happened to me yesterday!

Pat Oh? Tell me about it.

Ralf Well, I had a meeting in my office.

Pat Yes …

Ralf And when the meeting finished, I left the office to go for lunch. I wanted to try out that new Italian, you know the one.

Pat Go on …

Ralf So, anyway, I went down to the car park and I put my briefcase on top of the car and I took my coat off because the sun was shining. It was a beautiful day …

Pat Yes.

Ralf And I put my coat on the back seat of the car, closed the door, got in, and drove off.

Pat Where was your briefcase?

Ralf Well, that was the problem. I left it on the roof of the car.

Pat Oh no!

Ralf Yes. I drove all the way down the road, and then when I arrived at the restaurant I parked, and started looking for my briefcase.

Pat Because, of course, it wasn't on the roof of the car any more.

Ralf No, but just then my phone rang, so I answered it and it was a man who said he had my briefcase. So I got back in the car and drove back to the traffic lights where the man was waiting for me. He saw my bag fall off the car and picked it up.

Pat What did you say to him?

Ralf Well, I offered to give him some money, but he didn't want it, so I invited him for lunch.

Pat Did you go back to the Italian?

Ralf Yes, we did, the food was delicious! Anyway, while we were eating, the man said he didn't want any money, but he asked me to do him a favour.

Pat What did he ask you to do?

Ralf He gave me his CV. He said he was looking for a job, and he thought perhaps I could help him find one!

Pat So what did you do?

Ralf I promised to give his CV to some friends. Then we finished our lunch and said goodbye.

Pat You were really lucky he called you.

Ralf Yes, I know …

41.1

Jana I'm sorry?

Catherine My first name. It's with a 'C', not a 'K'.

Jana OK. I'll change that now.

Catherine Oh, and because it's a training session with lots of activities, thirty people will be too many.

Jana Oh, well, I'm still not sure of numbers … Is twenty-five OK, then?

Catherine Well. It's going to be very busy. But OK. Thank you. One more thing – I'm arriving on Thursday evening, and I'm staying at a hotel out of town, but my flight only arrives after 11.00 at night, so …um.

Jana So … the training starts too early?

Catherine Er… Yes. Can you move it?

Jana Shall I change it to 10.00 a.m.?

Catherine Oh, yes, please! But not for Saturday, because I'm flying back to England at 7.00 that evening.

Jana Oh, OK. So a ten o'clock start on Friday, but nine on Saturday?

Catherine Yes. Thanks.

41.2

Catherine About the um, the extras.

Jana Yes?

Catherine Well, are you providing a laptop for me?

listening script

Jana Yes. We've got one here. By the way, when can you send the handouts for photocopying?

Catherine Ah. Well, I'm working on the training course materials this week, so I'll send the handouts at the beginning of next week. Is that OK?

Jana Yes, fine.

Catherine Oh, and I'm going to set up some activities with the group, and there are a few things I can't bring. Um, some fresh eggs, about 200 paper clips, er, four balls of string, a packet of …

Jana Er, eggs, did you say?

Catherine Yes!

Jana OK. Look, please send me an email with all these things. I'll do my best to arrange them for you.

Catherine Oh, OK, I'll do that straight away.

Jana Right. Anything else?

Catherine Yes. I'm also going to need a packet of balloons.

Jana I see.

42.1

Ricky So, Sue, tell me about this guy, Carlton.

Sue OK, what do you want to know?

Ricky Where's he from?

Sue Denver, Colorado.

Ricky How old is he?

Sue Forty-eight.

Ricky What does he look like?

Sue Well, look, here are some photos.

Ricky Does he play electric or acoustic?

Sue Both.

Ricky Is he reliable?

Sue Absolutely. 100%.

Ricky Has he played in resorts before?

Sue Not much, he's done hotels and bars mainly.

Ricky Who writes his songs?

Sue He does himself, but he does covers too.

Ricky Has he recorded anything?

Sue Yes, but not commercially.

Ricky Have you brought a demo CD?

Sue Of course. Here, take a listen.

Ricky Can he play next month?

Sue Probably, it depends on the week.

42.2

Ricky Who wrote that song?

Sue He did. Carlton.

Ricky Did he? Hmm. All right, all right, I like the voice. I like the sound. Let's talk details.

Sue Good. When do you want him to play?

Ricky The third week of next month, from the 15th through the 21st.

Sue Was that the 16th to the 21st?

Ricky No, from the 15th. He is free, isn't he?

Sue Yeah, he is.

Ricky Could he play twice a night?

Sue Yeah, sure. Is forty-five minutes OK for each set of songs?

Ricky Fine, forty-five minutes is long enough.

Sue Would he be playing in the restaurant?

Ricky Yes, the first set in the restaurant and the second in the bar.

Sue Oh, how come?

Ricky The restaurant closes at eleven, but the bar's open all night.

Sue Fine. Er, Ricky, it's almost lunchtime. Shall we continue our conversation in a restaurant over lunch?

Ricky Yes, why not?

43.1

Beatrice Are you going to do a summer course?

Luca I suppose … but I don't know which one to do.

Beatrice I think I'll take the course in International Logistics.

Luca Logistics! But it's fifty hours!

Beatrice Yes, I know it's the longest course, but it's more important than the other two.

Luca Why?

Beatrice Because it has ten credits. It must be more important.

Luca Yes, but Logistics? I don't think Logistics is as interesting as Marketing and it's really expensive.

Beatrice Perhaps.

Luca Just a minute. €180 Marketing in China and … €120 for Advertising! That's €60 more expensive! Why's that? Why's the Advertising course cheaper than the other two?

Beatrice I don't know. The group is as big as the Marketing group. And the Marketing course is only one hour longer. I don't know. I don't understand. Just look at the price of the Logistics course!

Luca Yes. It's the most expensive one. €240.

Beatrice And the group is a lot bigger. Fifty people.

Luca Ah Beatrice, sometimes it's better to be in a bigger group! You don't get asked so many questions …

Beatrice Yes, you're right.

Luca I think I'll do Advertising!

Beatrice Why?

Luca It's the only course in the afternoon, Beatrice. Can you imagine getting up early in the morning to go to a lecture on Logistics or Marketing? After all, it is the summer!

Beatrice Well, I should do Logistics, really.

Luca Oh, come on, Beatrice! Why don't we do Advertising together? Then we can go out with the other students straight after the class. Come on …. Logistics in the morning or Advertising in the afternoon? What's it going to be?

Beatrice I don't know, Luca. I really don't know. I'll think about it and tell you tomorrow.

44.1

1 This book was printed in Portugal.
2 Your application for a visa is being processed.
3 The virus was first identified by a Dutch scientist.
4 Oranges are grown here.
5 A lot of books have been written about this period.
6 This pyramid was built around the year 2000 BC.
7 The bridge was opened by the President of France in 2005.
8 Iberia flight 413 to Bilbao has been cancelled due to bad weather.

44.2

Marga Sorry, what are you saying?

Bank Yes, there's a problem with one of the cheques that you banked last week. It's been refused by their bank.

Marga Refused? Why has it been refused?

Bank Yes, apparently the company doesn't have funds to cover the amount.

Marga Can you give me the details please?

Bank Certainly, the cheque was issued in the name of Open Enterprises Limited, and it was deposited by you on Friday last week. The amount is –

Marga Open Enterprises? Oh, I remember.

Bank And it was signed by, er, let me see … ah, Susan Weston.

Marga She must be new, but it's not the first time we've had problems with them.

Listening bank 01

Presenter How much do you know about the sudoku? Have you ever tried to do one? We asked Kieran Golding of Puzzles Publishing Ltd. to come to the studio and tell us more about them. Kieran, where does the sudoku come from?

Kieran Well, there are several theories. Some people say it's a version of the Latin Squares designed in 1783 by a Swiss mathematician called Leonhard Euler. But a New York puzzles magazine, *Dell*, also says they published the first sudokus under the name 'Number Place'.

Presenter But the name 'sudoku' is Japanese, isn't it?

Kieran Yes. A Japanese publisher, Maki Kaji, saw the Number Place puzzle, changed it a little and renamed it 'sudoku'. In Japanese 'su' means 'number' and 'doku' literally means, 'single' or 'only'. The puzzle became very popular in Japan during the nineteen-eighties.

Presenter So how did it spread to other countries?

Kieran By chance, really. A retired New Zealand judge called Wayne Gould found a book of them in a Tokyo bookshop and thought it would be possible to write a computer program to produce sudokus on the spot. Now, national newspapers in twelve different countries buy sudokus from him, although he says he hasn't made a lot of money from his program.

Presenter So most sudokus are produced by computer, are they?

Kieran Well, no actually. Maki Kaji is the president of a Japanese company called Nikoli and his company produces hand-written sudokus. Nikoli has sixteen employees supplying sudokus to all Japanese newspapers and magazines and some newspapers abroad. Nikoli has sold over two million puzzle books in Japan since 1988 and publishes sudoku books in about sixty countries as well.

Presenter I've heard that Nintendo are working on some new sudoku software to be published soon?

Kieran Yes, they are. And you can even go on a sudoku holiday.

Presenter I'm sorry? A sudoku holiday? You can't be serious!

Kieran Oh yes, I am. There's a castle in the north of France which is offering a sudoku break for addicts whose partners do not share their hobby. There's a giant sudoku in the garden of the castle and there's even a sudoku on the wall of the shower in each room!

Presenter But, are there really people who are so addicted that their idea of a holiday is a weekend doing sudokus?

Kieran Yes, there are. We receive thousands of emails every day from sudoku fans. One man once told us that he gets extremely depressed if he doesn't complete a sudoku puzzle before lunchtime.

Presenter So do sudokus have any educational value?

Kieran Apparently so. A leading education magazine has recommended teachers to use sudokus in the classroom as a useful brain exercise for their students. You have to concentrate to be able to solve a sudoku puzzle, and they're very motivating. I think they're great, both for adults and children.

Presenter Kieran Golding, thank you for talking to us.

Listening bank 02

Newsreader … the spokesman for the Bank of England said that interest rates are not expected to change in the next three months.

Presenter You will know the famous book by Jules Verne, *Around the World in Eighty Days* but how about *Around the World in 4,000 Days*? Some of you will recognize the name of Karl Bushby, the Englishman who is trying to set a unique world record. He wants to be the first man to walk around the world alone. He thinks the journey will take between ten and twelve years to complete. He will have to cross twenty-five countries, one frozen sea, six deserts, seven mountain ranges, and 36,000 miles, and all of them on foot.

Karl Bushby is now thirty-seven years old. After eleven years in the British Army he decided that he wanted to do something different, something that no other person had done before. He realized that he could walk non-stop from Punta Arenas in Chile, South America, to his home in Hull in England. With the help of his father and a close friend, Karl began what he calls the Goliath Expedition in November 1998. He has already completed seventeen thousand miles. He plans to return to England in the year 2009.

Karl walked all the way from Patagonia, crossing all of South, Central, and North America. He then waited for winter so that he could cross the Bering Sea between Alaska and Russia. After a difficult crossing of the frozen sea, with temperatures as low as minus thirty degrees centigrade, he finally entered Russian territory on the Chukchi Peninsula in April this year.

Unfortunately, the Russian authorities have arrested Karl for violation of frontier-crossing regulations. They say that Karl does not have the necessary documents to enter Russia and cannot enter the country. He is now waiting for the final decision about his situation. He hopes he will be allowed to continue. Karl has said that he doesn't know what he will do if the authorities say no.

At the moment Karl is waiting for news in the border village of Anadyr. Our Moscow correspondent sent this report.

Correspondent Karl Bushby, the intrepid British man who is trying to become the first person to walk around the world, is still waiting for news in the village of Anadyr in the Chukotka Autonomous region. He had completed half of his journey when the authorities stopped him from entering Russia. Nobody knows at the moment if he will be able to enter Russia and complete the second half of his journey through Siberia, Central Asia, and finally Western Europe, or if he will have to abandon and return to Britain. Mr Bushby is obviously very concerned about his situation but hopes that the final decision, which will not be made public for another ten days, will be in his favour. Jason Williams, Radio 5, Moscow.

Presenter If you would like more information about Karl's incredible journey you may like to read his book *Giant Steps* in which he describes his experiences in America, or you can visit his webpage, which is www.goliath.mail2web.com. That's w w w dot goliath dot mail2web dot com, where you can read his diary and see photographs of his adventure.

Listening bank 03

Monica Hello Dave. Great to see you! Did you have a good summer?

Dave Hi Monica. I had a fantastic time! How about you?

Monica Oh, quiet. I was with the family, visiting friends. But you obviously had a great time. You look really brown!

Dave Thanks – yeah, I've had a really good summer. I've been driving a taxi to earn some money.

Monica But you don't get brown from driving a taxi! So what have you been doing?

Dave Well, not exactly driving a taxi … riding one!

Monica Riding a taxi? What do you mean by riding a taxi?

Dave I'll tell you over coffee. Come on!

…

Monica So what have you been up to?

Dave Well, do you remember Jordi?

Monica Jordi? Ah yes! The student from Barcelona? Didn't he come here with Erasmus?

listening script

Dave That's right. He went back to Barcelona in June and he invited me to go over and spend some time with him there.

Monica Very nice.

Dave Yeah, so I went to Barcelona for a couple of weeks at the beginning of July. I thought it would be good for my Spanish… Have you ever been there?

Monica No, I haven't.

Dave You've just got to go. It's an incredible city. There's so much to do there.

Monica Oh! When are you going to tell me about the taxis?

Dave I'm coming to that. Well, I liked the place so much and my Spanish was really getting better, so I decided to stay all summer, but I needed money. At first I thought about a job in a bar or a restaurant, so I decided to rent a bike to get around the centre cheaply. I went to this place called Trixi where they rent bicycles to tourists and they gave me a job there.

Monica Renting bicycles?

Dave No, when I got there I saw all these special tricycles, you know the ones where two passengers can sit in the back and the rider sits at the front …

Monica In Barcelona?

Dave Yes. I asked the man at Trixi about them and he told me that they needed drivers who could speak languages well. I told him I spoke English, French, and Spanish and he gave me an interview. They phoned me the next day and offered me a job.

Monica But isn't that dangerous? Barcelona is a big place. There must be a lot of traffic.

Dave Yes, but you don't ride on the street at all. These special taxis can go anywhere a bicycle can go and there are lots of cycle paths and park areas in Barcelona. Trixi has permission to take passengers round all the sightseeing areas in the centre.

Monica But it must be hard work. Riding a bicycle with three people.

Dave Well, it is and it isn't. The taxis have a small electric motor to help you when you start pedalling but as soon as you're moving, I think when you're doing about eleven kilometres an hour, the electric motor stops. It's not as hard as it sounds. I'll show you some photographs tomorrow.

Monica How long did you work for them?

Dave Six weeks, until the end of August. I used to work about six hours every day. I had a great time!

Monica What? Riding a bicycle for six hours a day?

Dave Yes, seriously. The people at Trixi are really friendly. I got on really well with them and my French and Spanish have really improved.

Monica Did you get a lot of money?

Dave Not a lot, but enough to live on. I was staying in a hostel in the centre so I didn't need a lot of money, and I got some extra money from tips from the tourists as well.

Monica Well, you certainly look well. How many miles did you ride in total?

Dave I don't know in miles. I suppose on a busy day I did about sixty kilometres. Some days a lot less. Say forty kilometres a day on average so … about one and a half thousand kilometres, perhaps a bit more.

Monica I'm not surprised you've lost weight! How many other people were there working for Trixi?

Dave Quite a lot. There were people from all over the world, Spanish of course, and Italians, French, Germans, two English people like me, a girl from Australia …

Monica A girl?

Dave Yes, Jessica, really nice. She was really popular with everybody. She was staying in the same hostel as me.

Monica So you'll show me the photographs?

Dave Yes, I'll bring them tomorrow.

Monica Have you got any photos of Jessica?

Dave Yes, one or two. Why?

Listening bank 04

Interviewer When did you first want to fly planes?

Ildikó Well, when I was a child, my father used to take me to the airport to watch the planes taking off and landing, and I imagined that one day I could be a pilot too. But really it was just a dream.

Interviewer What was your first job?

Ildikó Well, at school, I wanted to be a vet, you know, a doctor for animals. I love animals, but I wasn't good at maths or physics, and I needed those for university, so studying to be a vet was out of the question. So instead I studied music at the Academy in Budapest. It was the most natural thing for me to do, because my family is quite musical.

Interviewer That's quite different from being a vet! Did you then go into music as a career?

Ildikó Oh no! I got a job at Hungarian TV in the co-production department. My job was to develop contacts with TV companies abroad. It was great, especially because it wasn't a typical eight-to-four job, and I was able to travel, and used my French, German, and Italian for work. In those days, it wasn't easy for Hungarians to travel abroad.

Interviewer But what about flying?

Ildikó Well, whenever I travelled by plane, I always went to the cockpit with questions for the pilot. There was one trip when I was returning from Paris, and I decided I just had to learn how to fly. In my heart, that's what I really wanted to do. We were on a Tupolyev plane, a Russian plane, one of my favourites. And in those days I thought the pilots were like gods – I respected them so much! Anyway, the captain of the plane explained to me how to become a pilot. He told me about a flying club just outside Budapest.

Interviewer And did you go?

Ildikó Yes, of course! I thought I could just learn to glide and become a private pilot, but this was in 1989, and there weren't private pilots then. You weren't allowed to fly just for fun.

Interviewer Were there any other women flying then?

Ildikó No, none! So they were all a bit surprised at the flying club. But in the end I went so often that they believed me. I spent the first year gliding, and then after a year I tried a one-engine power plane.

Interviewer But what about your job in TV?

Ildikó Well, in the end I had to give that up. I was there for eighteen months, but it was too difficult to travel in and out of town all the time. But I also thought I should get a job more closely related to flying. So I decided to become an air hostess. That was good, because I was close to the cockpit. I still asked questions, but I learnt a lot. I used to listen in to the pilots' radio telephoning and hear all their special flying language. And I saw airports from the air – it was amazing.

Interviewer And did you still want to be a pilot?

Ildikó Yes, very much. But it took me nine years to become a passenger plane pilot. Usually it only takes four or five years, but, being a girl, it wasn't easy. I had to prove myself, and no one took me seriously. I was the only female at the time who wanted to be a professional pilot.

Interviewer You've now been a captain for one year, Hungary's first female captain!

Ildikó   Yes, well, two years ago I had the choice of transferring to a bigger plane, or flying the same planes and becoming a captain. At the moment I fly Dutch planes, the Fokker 70. For eight years now I've been flying those.

Interviewer   What extra skills do you need to be a captain?

Ildikó   Well, first, you have to do a minimum of one thousand five hundred flying hours. I actually did about three or four thousand hours. You see, I had to show them that I was capable. It wasn't easy! In practice in the air, the captain and the first officer do the same thing, really. But a captain needs good communication skills, leadership skills, and so on. We fly one leg of the return trip each. The pilot who is not flying does the radio telephoning, and gives instructions. But in the end, the captain is responsible for all the decisions that are made.

Interviewer   What about working with the other pilots? They're mostly men, aren't they?

Ildikó   Yes, but most of them are younger than me. But it's a great team.

Interviewer   Would you still like to fly something bigger?

Ildikó   Er, maybe. But bigger planes mean longer trips, and I have a lot of animals at home – seven cats, four dogs, and three goats. At the moment, I fly only within Europe, so I'm never away for long.

Interviewer   So would you still like to be a vet?

Ildikó   No, not really. But I have just finished a part-time four-year course in Forestry and Wildlife. But that was just for fun. I wanted to prove to myself that I could do it, and it was great. But I only want to fly now. I don't want to change careers again.

Interviewer   It sounds great. Ildikó, thank you!

Listening bank 05

Presenter   Good evening and welcome to this evening's programme of World Travel. The first part of this week's programme looks at the expanding world of low-cost airline companies. Companies such as easyJet, Ryanair, or Vueling in Spain have been operating since 1992 and the number of European cities now connected by these airlines is growing day by day. How is it possible that their prices are so low? We spoke to Harriet Goodson, a travel consultant for the Whitney Group.

Harriet   Low-cost airlines are becoming more and more popular simply because they offer a cheap way to travel. They offer a reasonable service at a much lower price than the established companies. This morning I looked on the Internet and saw a single flight from London Stansted to Amsterdam advertised for 17p. 17p! That's less than what I pay for a cup of coffee at the office!

Presenter   How do they do it?

Harriet   I think there are two main reasons. The first is that they have much lower costs than the bigger airlines. They only operate on profitable and popular routes. They don't use the major airports, which are very expensive, and they don't have an expensive infrastructure of offices and people all over the country because everything or almost everything is done on the Internet. I think that's the second main reason. Enquiries, reservations, cancellations – everything is done on the Internet from your home or office. They don't need offices.

Presenter   The number of people now travelling by air is ten times what it was fifteen years ago. Is this because of low-cost airlines?

Harriet   Yes, of course! More and more people are travelling by air and in the past it was quite normal to fly only once a year. Now many people are flying several times a year. In fact many ecologists say that this is becoming a major cause of pollution and global warming.

…

Presenter   Tom Blake of Liverpool is one of these people. He flies with easyJet up to twenty times a year. We asked him why.

Tom   My brother lives in Spain, not far from Alicante. Before, I went to Spain to visit him once a year and I never went with the family because it was too expensive. Now I can fly from Liverpool to Murcia airport, which isn't very far from where my brother lives, for as little as forty pounds there and back. I go every month for the weekend and I take all the family at Christmas and Easter. It's fantastic! I book the ticket on the Internet from home and I've never had any problems at all. It's great!

…

Presenter   But Margaret Wallace from Cambridge has a different story to tell.

Margaret   I like to travel by air. All my friends told me that I should fly with one of these low-cost companies. They said I was wasting my money buying my tickets at the travel agency. So I thought I would try. I booked my tickets for a weekend trip to Amsterdam. The return ticket only cost thirty-five pounds, which wasn't bad, but then I had to pay airport taxes, special insurance, and so on. The final price came to sixty-seven pounds, but that was still a lot cheaper than the normal price. Well, the flight was at seven o'clock in the morning! When I got to the airport there was a long queue of people waiting for the flight. We were delayed by nearly two hours. The plane was full of all these football supporters going to see a match. Then I had to pay nearly three pounds for a cup of tea and a biscuit! It wasn't for me! I didn't like it at all. I prefer to pay a little more but to have better service.

Presenter   So, two different opinions about low-cost travel. But if you can reserve your ticket on the Internet two or three months before you travel, and if the time of the flight is not important for you, then you should check the possibilities of low-cost airlines. Just one word of caution. Low-cost airlines are not always cheaper than their competitors, especially if you book your ticket a short time before you fly. Always compare prices before you buy. And now we listen to Jonathan Evans who has just returned from a trekking holiday in the Atlas Mountains …

Listening bank 06

Interviewer   There's a lot of talk about wind power these days. Tell us about it.

Expert   Well, in the nineteen-eighties, people were becoming interested in a more self-sufficient and independent lifestyle. They didn't want to rely on the oil and electricity provided by others. And of course there was also the oil crisis then too. People began to worry, and started thinking about other types of energy. They tried solar energy, but that's expensive, and this provides direct energy, energy which you can use immediately. But the new windmills you see these days, they provide indirect energy – energy which can be stored and used later. They're also sometimes called wind turbines. But let's call them windmills.

Interviewer   I see. OK.

Expert   Wind technology is now very well developed. In Europe, the energy we get from wind is about two thirds of the total wind power supply worldwide. The growth rate has been fantastic, and now wind

listening script

power costs only about a quarter of what it used to.

Interviewer   That's amazing! Some people say that windmills aren't very efficient. Why do you think wind power is so good?

Expert   Well, most importantly windmills don't use any other energy to make them work, and they don't produce any harmful by-products. So they're good for the environment. The other thing that's very important is that, at the moment, Europe gets about fifty percent of its energy, you know, gas, oil, and so on, from other countries, and there is a limit to what is available. So we need to find other ways of making energy.

Interviewer   How big are the windmills?

Expert   They vary a lot in size. Obviously the bigger ones are more effective, and the wind is stronger higher up. A windmill usually has three blades. On most windmills, the blades are about twenty metres long, so you have a diameter of about forty metres. But some of the larger windmills have much longer blades, with a rotor diameter of maybe eighty or ninety meters. The tower is usually about two or three times higher than the length of the blades. Inside the tower there is a ladder or even a lift in the bigger ones.

Interviewer   How much energy does a windmill produce?

Expert   A windmill needs an average wind speed of twenty-four kilometres an hour, per annum. In ideal wind conditions, one large windmill, like some of the ones in Austria, can produce, in a day, enough energy for an average family of four people for about three years.

Interviewer   That sounds a lot! But what if there's no wind?

Expert   Well, if the wind drops to less than eight kilometres an hour, then the windmill stops moving. And if there is too much wind, it stops working automatically.

Interviewer   How much land do you need to build a windmill?

Expert   One windmill needs about a quarter of a hectare, that's 2,500 square metres. The land shouldn't be too hilly. The best place for windmills is along the coast, or on high ground. That's why wind energy is so successful in Denmark, Germany, and the UK, because these countries have long coastlines. Poland has good windmill business, too. But you also need to get planning permission.

Interviewer   And is that difficult?

Expert   Well, that's the most difficult part. You need local government permission, and permission from a number of other local organizations. It can take up to a year. And then, on top of that, the local public can complain too. You need a lot of patience!

Interviewer   But the windmills sound great. Why do they complain?

Expert   Oh, all sorts of reasons. Some people say that they are noisy. Others say that they interfere with mobile phone connections. But the new windmills don't cause either of these problems any more. In Cumbria, in the north west of England, they worry about tourism because they say that the windmills are very ugly. You see, that part of the UK is quite high, and it's also near the coast, so it's very popular with tourists who go walking. But it's also ideal for windmills. It's true, the windmills make the countryside look different, but they are actually very elegant and quite beautiful.

Interviewer   Are birds and animals in any danger from windmills?

Expert   Well, this is really why it's sometimes very difficult to get permission. You can't build a windmill near to a nature reserve where there are animals. But it's much more difficult to decide where the birds are, you know, where they fly. The RSPB – the organization that looks after the birds' interests – do a lot of research into where large numbers of birds fly. It's obviously particularly important in coastal areas where people want to build wind farms, because that's where the wind is strong. And that's exactly what birds like, because then they can fly more quickly when they fly south, you know, when they migrate. But it's a real danger if they fly into the path of a windmill, and get caught in one of the blades. So the RSPB very often say 'no' to a wind farm proposal if it's planned for a route which is used by birds. But otherwise, they are very keen to promote different sources of energy – wind, solar, and so on, and they are also strong supporters of the Government's targets.

Interviewer   Uh huh. And what are the targets?

Expert   Well, the current UK target is that by 2015, fifteen per cent of all energy is from renewable sources. And wind power plays an important role in this.

Interviewer   And are they on target?

Expert   Well, overall, yes! In fact, Europe, as a whole, reached the EU 2010 targets five years early, in 2005. There is a lot of enthusiasm for wind power among European governments because of its obvious benefits for the environment and the economy.

LB06